13
Things Mentally Strong People Don't Do
WORKBOOK

Also by Amy Morin, LCSW

13
Things Mentally Strong People Don't Do
WORKBOOK

AMY MORIN, LCSW

WILLIAM MORROW
An Imprint of HarperCollins*Publishers*

HarperCollins books may be purchased for educational, business, or sales promotional use. For information, please email the Special Markets Department at SPsales@harpercollins.com.

FIRST EDITION

Designed by Diahann Sturge

Chapter opener stop sign art © TotemArt / Shutterstock
Check box art throughout © vectorplus / Shutterstock

Library of Congress Cataloging-in-Publication Data has been applied for.

ISBN 978-0-06-325223-3

23 24 25 26 27 LBC 5 4 3 2 1

To all those who know pain,
understand struggle,
and doubt their strength

Contents

13

Things Mentally Strong People Don't Do

WORKBOOK

Introduction

I LIVED THE first half of my life like it was a race. I spent my time checking off as many boxes as I could as if I expected to win a prize for achieving my goals as quickly as possible. By the time I was twenty-three, I was married, I had a house, I was a foster parent, and I had landed my first big job as a therapist. I thought the hard part was over—getting through college, finding an amazing life partner, and launching my career.

But then I got one of those phone calls that changes your life in an instant. My sister called to say our mom had been rushed to the hospital by ambulance. I was too confused to get any details about what had happened. As soon as I hung up, I jumped into the car with my husband, Lincoln, and we drove the hour and a half to the hospital. When we arrived, the doctor informed us my mother had a brain aneurysm that had ruptured and she'd passed away.

As a therapist I knew a thing or two about loss, but my education on grief did nothing for the sick feeling in my stomach that wouldn't go away. The person who had brought me into the world was no longer here and life felt somewhat empty without her.

I remember thinking, "OK, I have all these tools I recommend to people in my therapy office. Which ones am I going to reach for to help me work through my pain?" I kept thinking about how so many of my therapy clients grew from their painful experiences. But, I also knew some of them felt stuck in their pain.

When I thought about what separated people who grew from those who felt stuck, I realized it had to do with their habits. But, it wasn't always about what people did. Instead, it seemed to be more about what people *didn't* do. People who didn't have certain unhealthy habits seemed to be able to reach their greatest potential despite whatever challenges life threw their way.

Once I realized this, I wanted to ensure I was avoiding those unhealthy habits in my own life as I worked through my grief. But I also wanted to share that information with my clients. As a therapist, however, I'd been taught to build on people's strengths. I was supposed to point out what they were doing well already and encourage them to keep doing those things.

But I felt like I would be doing them a disservice if I didn't point out the counterproductive bad habits that were draining them of mental strength. So I closely studied what those habits were in order to help people eliminate the things that were keeping them stuck in life.

I am glad I worked on building mental strength and eliminating my unhealthy habits, because my tough times didn't end with the loss of my mom. On the three-year anniversary of the death of my mom, Lincoln said he didn't feel well. A few minutes later he collapsed.

I called an ambulance. They arrived within minutes, because the hospital was just down the street. The paramedics kept asking me over and over what had happened. I assured them he wasn't allergic to anything, he didn't use drugs, and he didn't have any serious health issues. They loaded him into the ambulance and I called Lincoln's mom as I got into the car to follow.

She met me in the hospital waiting room. I kept hoping Lincoln was just having some sort of allergic reaction or a health issue that could easily be fixed.

Finally, a nurse called us out back and for a second, I felt relieved because I thought we'd get to see Lincoln. But rather than take us to an exam room, she ushered us into a private room that looked like a closet with a table. I used to work at this hospital and I knew this wasn't the room where they shared good news. As we sat down, a doctor walked in and quickly said, "I'm sorry to tell you, but Lincoln has passed away." With that one sentence, life as I knew it came to a screeching halt.

The next week felt like a blur as we made plans for a funeral. And everyone wanted to know what had happened. It took a few weeks before we got confirmation that Lincoln had died of a heart attack. Whenever anyone asked me how I was doing, all I could say was, "It hurts to breathe." I didn't have any other way to explain how I felt and to say I felt bad felt like an understatement.

My company gave me a few days of bereavement leave, but clearly that wasn't enough. I saw my doctor and was diagnosed with acute stress disorder (the precursor to post-traumatic stress disorder), a determination that earned me the right to tap into my short-term disability so I could take paid leave from work. I was grateful for the time off because I wasn't in any shape to help other people manage their emotional turmoil when I was in the depths of despair.

I made a conscious decision to work through my grief—not go around the pain. Grief is the process by which we heal, even though it's a slow, painful experience. It was the darkest, loneliest, saddest three months of my life.

When I returned to work, I was far from healed. But I was a bit more prepared to get back to the office and get into a routine again. Eventually, I resumed some of the activities Lincoln and I had done together—like going back to being a foster parent. And slowly, I abandoned some of the dreams we'd had together—like adopting a child

It took years to build a new life and heal my broken heart. Occasionally, someone would ask about whether I was interested in dating again and my answer had always been no. I couldn't imagine dating anyone, let alone ever getting remarried. All that changed, though, when I met Steve. He is the kindest, most patient human I've ever met. And being with him just feels right.

We fell in love and got married—at a drive-through wedding chapel in Las Vegas in a 1957 Chevy Bel Air. It was a fun way to kick off our new life. We bought a house together in a different area. I landed a new job. And I felt grateful that I was able to get a fresh start in life.

But shortly after we were married we got word that my father-in-law had cancer. Initially, the doctors said they thought his cancer was treatable. But after a few weeks, they said it was spreading and there was nothing they could do. They gave him a grim prognosis—three months to live.

When I heard that news, I thought, "No, I can't go through this again. I spent the last decade grieving. I don't have it in me to grieve anymore." I didn't think I could handle another loss, but it wasn't like I had a choice.

That all-too-familiar sick feeling in my stomach returned. Unlike when I'd lost my mother and Lincoln suddenly and unexpectedly, though, this time I knew what was coming. And I started to feel sorry for myself. My father-in-law was one of my biggest fans and he and I had grown close. I had started doing a little freelance writing on the side and he always called to ask me what I was working on. And he always had the best jokes and the most mind-boggling magic tricks.

But I knew that feeling sorry for myself wasn't going to help. In fact, it was one of those things that would drain me of mental strength if I let it. So I sat down and I wrote myself a letter that included all of the things mentally strong people don't do, based on what I'd learned in my therapy office and throughout my previous experiences with loss.

When I was done, I had a list of 13 things. I read that list every day—sometimes multiple times—and found it helpful. I then decided to publish it online, hoping it might help someone else, and expected that it might be read by just a handful of people. I never imagined it would go viral and be read by more than 50 million people!

Just three days after his death, a national news show interviewed me on live TV. The same day, I met with a literary agent who suggested I write a book. Within a month, I had a book deal. It was a surreal experience. As I was publicly celebrating the success of my article, I was privately grieving the loss of my father-in-law.

I almost didn't make my list public. It was a private letter to myself. I certainly never imagined it would turn into a book. But one year later, *13 Things Mentally Strong People Don't Do* hit the shelves. And it was beyond my wildest dreams that my books would sell over a million copies and be translated into more than forty languages.

A lot has changed since I wrote that letter to myself. I took a break from seeing clients in my therapy office so I could have more time to write. And I wrote three more books—*13 Things Mentally Strong Parents Don't Do*, *13 Things Mentally Strong Women Don't Do*, and *13 Things Strong Kids Do*. I also gave a TEDx Talk titled "The Secret of Becoming Mentally Strong" that has been viewed more than twenty-one million times.

I became the editor in chief of Verywell Mind, the biggest mental health site in the world. I also launched *The Verywell Mind Podcast*, in which I get to interview celebrities, authors, and experts about their best tips for staying mentally strong, and share my favorite strategies for building mental strength. I talk about a lot of the same things I used to talk about in my therapy office. But now I get to do it on a much bigger scale.

I also give a lot of speeches—something I never imagined I'd do, since public speaking used to feel terrifying. Now I stand on stages in front of thousands of people and talk about mental strength. I love that I get to do that.

My personal life has changed a lot too. Steve and I moved from Maine to the Florida Keys, where we live full-time on a sailboat. I still go back to Maine often to visit my friends and family, and Lincoln's family remains a big part of my life.

Life has become a wild, beautiful adventure. I wish I never had to go through such tough times to get here, but it's an honor to share my journey and what I'm learning along the way.

The world has changed a lot too since my book hit the shelves in 2013. We're a lot more comfortable talking about mental health and mental strength now. Therapy has become normalized, and it's much more common for people to talk about the importance of caring for their minds.

Readers often ask me, "Were you always mentally strong?" I smile when I hear that question because I struggled with mental strength for most of my life. I was an anxious kid who actually vomited before school sometimes up until I was in the fourth grade. I never spoke in front of my class—not even in high school, because public speaking felt too scary. I was a perfectionist, I hated change, I was scared of being judged, and I avoided doing anything outside my comfort zone.

I am still a work in progress, but if I learned anything along the way, it's that I am capable of building mental strength.

Mental strength isn't something you either have or you don't. It's something you need to build with exercise. To get the most out of these exercises, you also need to get rid of the unhealthy habits that rob you of mental strength.

Developing mental muscle is a lot like developing physical muscle. To get physically stronger, you need to exercise. And if you really want to see results, you need to get rid of counterproductive bad habits like eating too much junk food.

That's where this workbook comes in. It's based on the same principles in my original book. But I've expanded on the information with more actionable strategies, questions, and exercises that will give you a step-by-step guide to creating your own mental muscle building plan.

Benefits of Building Mental Strength

Right about now you might be thinking that building mental strength requires too much work—and strength you don't yet have. But don't let your brain talk you out of doing what it takes to grow stronger.

This book contains some quick tips that can give fast relief from your distress. It also offers plenty of exercises you can start incorporating into your daily life so you can build mental muscle for the long haul.

When you grow stronger, you'll feel better. You'll also be able to do things you couldn't once do. But don't just take it from me. Here's what a few readers say:

Now that I'm mentally stronger, I can . . .

LOVE MYSELF and others more effectively. I can understand that people's behaviors are a reflection of them, not of me. I can approach situations with kindness and compassion, even in the face of adversity. And I can help other people live their truths as well.

—Lance Kelly (35, Pennsylvania)

BE A BETTER PERSON to myself. Maybe more important, a better person to the important people in my life.

—Dave (59, Michigan)

HAVE GREATER CONFIDENCE going forward. Mental strength translates to more peace in the everyday and less anxiety.

—Casey Morlet (36, California)

TAKE CARE OF MYSELF and my needs, focus on the good, and stay optimistic and positive.

—Heidi Croft (43, Utah)

BE AT PEACE with the fact that I can do all the "right" things, and someone will still have a problem with me. I went through a very difficult year at work in 2020, but it led me to have some uncomfortable conversations with people and now things are better. But most of all, I don't attach my value as a person to what other people think of me.

—Ashley (29, Oregon)

ALLOW MYSELF PERMISSION to have opinions that differ from others and be OK when things around me aren't OK.

—Amy Woodley (36, Canada)

ENCOURAGE OTHER PEOPLE more effectively, navigate conflict better, and in general weather the storms of life with more confidence.

—April Spicer (43, Indiana)

BE MORE AUTHENTIC and not so self-conscious about my flaws, or what people might be thinking about me. I'm more present for others as well, and not so "in my own head" all the time.

—Sarah Thomas (37, Oregon)

MAKE MORE EFFECTIVE DECISIONS, both personally and professionally.

—Vanessa (52, New York)

BE HAPPY in the now while I still strive to accomplish my future goals. The past is still there; I no longer dwell over it but simply learn from it.

—Jason Smith (35, Colorado)

The Three Parts of Mental Strength

Over the years, I have heard a lot of misconceptions about mental strength. Sometimes people say things like, "I can't be mentally strong because I have depression," or "You didn't cry today. That means you're getting stronger." Neither of those things is accurate.

Mental strength isn't the same thing as mental health. Think of it like physical health and physical strength. You can lift weights to get physically stronger. And developing some physical strength is good for your physical health. But it doesn't guarantee that you won't ever develop a physical health issue like high cholesterol.

The same can be said for mental strength. You can choose to work out your mind, but it doesn't guarantee you won't ever develop a mental health issue like depression. Bigger mental muscles can prevent some mental health issues, but developing a mental health issue isn't a sign of weakness. In fact, some of the strongest people I've ever met were battling things like depression or anxiety.

Keep in mind that "not crying" also isn't a hallmark of mental strength. Becoming mentally stronger doesn't involve suppressing your emotions or acting like nothing bothers you. In fact, it's quite the opposite. It takes a fair amount of mental strength to allow yourself to experience and express uncomfortable feelings—that's something that we'll talk more about throughout this workbook.

There are three parts of mental strength: thoughts, feelings, and behavior. They're intertwined and you'll find that when you change one part, the other two things shift. Here's an example:

 Thought—"No one is going to talk to me at this party."

 Feeling—Nervous and sad

 Behavior—Sits in the corner alone and leaves early

In this scenario, an individual's thoughts and negative predictions are likely to become a self-fulfilling prophecy. They're likely to behave in a way that ensures no one talks to them, which reinforces their belief that no one will like them.

If, however, that same person responded to a negative thought with a healthier one, they might be able to change the outcome. Here's an example:

 Thought: "I'm going to introduce myself to five new people."

 Feeling: Nervous and excited

 Behavior: Introduces self to people and enjoys friendly conversation all evening

Responding to unhelpful thoughts is just one way to attack a negative cycle like this. Sometimes it's important to take charge of your emotions. At other times, you can change your behavior to test your negative thoughts. Each chapter that follows is filled with exercises that can help you break free from unhealthy patterns that are keeping you stuck in life. We'll combat each unhealthy habit with strategies that change the ways you think, feel, and behave.

How to Use This Book

The original *13 Things* book focuses on what "*they* don't do." But this workbook is about *you*. By the time you finish this book, you'll have the tools and skills you need to put your unhealthy habits behind you.

To be clear, it's not that mentally strong people don't ever do these things. We all do them sometimes. Learning to recognize your unhealthy habits and the strategies that combat them will make your healthy habits much more effective.

You don't need to go through this workbook in order, however. If there's a specific "thing" you struggle with, or something you want to focus on first, feel free to skip ahead. But I encourage you to go through all the chapters eventually, because each one contains different mental strength exercises that can work in a variety of situations.

Once you dive into certain chapters, you also might find that they resonate with you more than you predicted. I have had countless readers over the years say things like, "I didn't think I was a people pleaser until I got into that chapter!"

Also, keep in mind that just because you don't struggle with something now doesn't mean it won't ever become a problem for you. It's easy to avoid feeling sorry for yourself when life is going well. But it can be much more difficult to avoid the self-pity trap when you lose your job or you're going through a rough breakup. Doing the work ahead of time will equip you with the knowledge and tools to face those hard situations.

The mental strength exercises in this book aren't just for getting through or preparing for tough times, though. It'd be awful to think that the only reason you need mental strength is so that you can prepare yourself for tragedy. Mental strength is also key to helping you enjoy the good times. Growing stronger will help you get the most out of life.

And even if you feel you have mastered a skill, reinforcing what you already know never hurts. You might find it's helpful to reflect on the things you're doing well in order to build your confidence. You might also recognize opportunities to apply the skills you already have to new areas of your life.

In each chapter, you'll find:

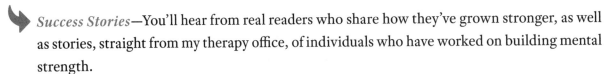 *Success Stories*—You'll hear from real readers who share how they've grown stronger, as well as stories, straight from my therapy office, of individuals who have worked on building mental strength.

Quizzes—Quizzes will help you identify the unhealthy habits that are robbing you of mental strength, why you engage in them, and what you can do differently.

Reflection Questions—Throughout the book, you'll find questions that will help you better understand yourself and the steps you can take to create positive change. You might be tempted to skip these or just answer them in your head. Don't do it. Writing your thoughts down is a powerful way to create change. You'll also be able to look back over the progress you've made and the lessons you've learned when you have written down your thoughts.

Mental Strength Exercises—Every chapter contains several mental strength–building exercises that you can begin practicing right now.

This Week's Homework—Each chapter contains an exercise that you can start incorporating into your everyday life. I'll explain how you can practice it as you go about your week.

 Plan for Change—At the end of each chapter, you'll create a plan that will help you develop your own step-by-step guide for creating lasting change.

While the exercises are many of the same strategies I have used with my therapy clients, this book isn't a substitute for mental health treatment. Clearly, however, individual therapy isn't easily accessible to everyone. And if the pandemic taught us anything, it's that mental strength is something we should all be concerned with.

Reading this book won't change your life. But putting the exercises into practice could. It's up to you to put the knowledge into action. I'll show you how to do that so you can become the strongest and best version of yourself.

Before we get started, let's get clear on what you hope to accomplish. What do you want to achieve by building mental strength?

_____

_____

_____

_____

_____

_____

_____

_____

_____

_____

_____

_____

_____

When I **STOPPED** feeling sorry for myself . . .

I understood that in life I play no victim. No one is up there grounding me or punishing me for eternal bad luck. It's just life the way it is and I cannot change it. However, I can shift my thinking and take action and make things work better for me.

—Enrique Vazquez (31, Mexico)

I ran out of excuses for all the reasons why my life wasn't going well. Then I was free to take charge and make things better.

—Rachel Hamilton (38, Connecticut)

I started to enjoy life. Instead of wallowing in self-pity, I took action and felt grateful.

—Josh Fletcher (27, Utah)

Don't Waste Time Feeling Sorry for Yourself

I WAS FEELING sorry for myself when I wrote that original letter to myself about what mentally strong people don't do. I was thinking about all the reasons why I shouldn't have to deal with one more loss in my life. I was so busy convincing myself I wasn't capable of dealing with more grief that I wasn't working on myself.

That's why "don't feel sorry for yourself" tops the list—it was the "thing" I was struggling with most at that moment.

Many readers have said this chapter struck a chord with them. Some said they had developed a lifelong pattern of feeling sorry for themselves, while others said they thought self-pity was a natural response to emotional pain. One reader emailed me and said, "For a long time I had to ensure my life stayed miserable. It was the only way I could justify my addiction. I needed to create a 'bad life' so I could have excuses about why I needed to reach for another drink."

Other readers express a bit of anger about the suggestion that self-pity is voluntary. Some of them don't understand the distinction between sadness and self-pity. Others think their self-pity is justified—at least until they choose to address it. I understand where this frustration comes from. After all, sometimes it's not just our perception that life is difficult. Life really is difficult! We'll talk more about that a little later in the book, but no matter how bad things are, I promise, self-pity will only make it worse.

How Do You Feel Sorry for Yourself?

We all feel sorry for ourselves sometimes. But we do so for different reasons and in different ways. In this chapter, we'll cover how to recognize when you're falling into the self-pity trap and the strategies that can help. But first, let's get started by examining the ways in which you might feel sorry for yourself. Place a checkmark next to the following statements that sound like you.

☐ I avoid my problems, rather than address them.

☐ I complain to people who don't have the ability to solve the problem.

☐ I insist my problems are worse than everyone else's.

☐ When people offer solutions, I insist they won't work for me without even trying.

☐ I don't bother trying to change my life because I assume nothing is going to work.

☐ I tell myself I am justified in feeling self-pity because my life is so bad.

☐ I sit around thinking about my problems instead of taking action.

☐ I feel hopeless and helpless.

What's a time when you felt sorry for yourself? Describe the circumstances.

_____

_____

_____

_____

_____

What were some of the thoughts you had during this time?

_____

_____

_____

_____

How did self-pity affect your behavior? What did you do?

_____

_____

_____

_____

Feeling Sad vs. Feeling Self-Pity

Self-pity (which is the same as feeling sorry for yourself) is different from sadness.

Sadness can help you honor something important that you miss having in your life—a loved one, a job, or an activity, for example. It can also help you honor a dream you've let go of—such as the life you thought you were going to have.

Self-pity, however, causes you to stay stuck in a state of misery. It involves focusing on the unfairness of the situation. It exaggerates your misfortune and prevents you from taking positive action.

Here are some examples of the different types of thoughts you have when you're feeling sad versus when you're feeling self-pity:

FEELING SAD	SELF-PITY
It would be nice to have someone to hang out with tonight.	No one likes me. Everyone else has friends and fun stuff to do. I always get left out.
I am sad I didn't get that job.	I'll never get a better job. I'm going to be stuck in this position forever.
Most of my plans are going to need to change now that I'm getting a divorce.	I'll never get back on my feet financially after the divorce. My life is ruined.

What's a time when you felt healthy sadness (even though it hurt)?

_____

_____

_____

_____

_____

What are some of the thoughts you had when you felt healthy sadness?

_____

_____

_____

_____

_____

What did you do to take care of your sad feelings?

_____

_____

_____

_____

_____

When Do You Feel Sorry for Yourself?

> I found myself with a large personal financial obligation that I refused to walk away from. "I borrowed the money. I will pay it back, regardless of how hard it would be." That's just who I am. I spent a little time on occasion feeling sorry for myself every once in a while. Even though I didn't waste much time on feeling sorry for myself, I soon realized that I could have—and, should have—been using that time for thinking on solutions, either increasing income or reducing obligations . . . ideally, both.
>
> —Dan Durishan (63, Delaware)

Everyone has different triggers that lead to self-pity. While one person might feel sorry for themselves when they dislike their job, another might host a pity party when they experience a social rejection. Which events or circumstances are most likely to cause you to feel sorry for yourself?

☐ When I get rejected for something in my professional life

☐ When I feel lonely

☐ When I encounter an unexpected obstacle

☐ When other people talk about their good fortune

☐ When I feel disappointed

☐ When I fail at something

☐ When my feelings are hurt

☐ When I feel rejected by a love interest

☐ _____

My Warning Signs

You might feel sorry for yourself sometimes without realizing it. Self-pity might creep up on you slowly over time. Or it might seem justified in the moment, making it difficult to recognize.

So it's important to know your personal warning signs that you're starting to feel sorry for yourself. Which of these things do you likely do when you are hosting a pity party?

- ☐ Complain to multiple people
- ☐ Binge-watch TV
- ☐ Waste time scrolling through my phone
- ☐ Isolate myself from others
- ☐ Think about the unfairness of my situation
- ☐ Insist no one understands me
- ☐ Turn down healthy activities
- ☐ Reach for unhealthy coping skills (like food, alcohol, or social media)
- ☐ _____

> *I found that feeling sorry for myself would distract me from what's PRESENT in my life. I would feel sorry for myself, and that would stop me from moving forward . . . from finding a solution . . . from having a mindset of "How to . . ." rather than a mindset of "Why me?"*
>
> —Steve Gonzalez (57, Pennsylvania)

Anna started therapy by saying that she needed help reducing the stress in her life. She said she was motivated to create some serious changes. But at each subsequent appointment, she didn't want to talk about anything she could do differently. Instead, she wanted to talk about all the bad things that had happened in the past week.

This seemed to be a theme in her communication patterns outside my therapy office too. She reported bad news as often as she could.

She sent text messages to her friends on a daily basis that said things like, "You're not going to believe how awful today was!" She then listed everything that went wrong that day, such as being yelled at by a customer and having to wait twenty minutes for her ride. She never told them anything good that happened.

Part of her homework involved logging her communication so she could look for patterns. After just a couple of weeks she realized that she found some twisted joy in sharing bad news because it gave her an excuse to feel sorry for herself. She also realized that she was essentially inviting her friends to join her pity party by announcing her misfortunes on a daily basis. She hoped by telling them how awful things were, she could get attention, gain sympathy, and receive their blessing for not creating any positive changes in her life.

Through talk therapy, she discovered that she secretly hoped other people would reinforce her decision to stay stuck. She said, "I don't want advice or even support. Instead, I want people to recognize that I have bad luck and shouldn't be expected to do much with my life." Compiling a list of "bad news" items strengthened her belief that she shouldn't bother to work on anything because "bad things" always seemed to happen anyway. By all means, she had endured some rough patches in life, but she wasn't doomed to keep suffering.

Through treatment, she recognized the downside to self-pity too. She was a "downer" to her friends. And she knew she certainly wasn't living her best life.

One of the many exercises we worked on in treatment involved gratitude. She began looking for good things in her life and practiced talking about positive things. At first, it felt a bit uncomfortable. Sharing good things felt like bragging. But over time, she noticed that sharing good things about her life boosted her mood and inspired healthier conversations.

We also worked on changing BLUE thoughts into true thoughts—an exercise you'll learn in just a minute. This helped her recognize how she often convinced herself that minor inconveniences were major obstacles in life. She learned how to talk back to her unhelpful, negative thoughts so she could feel a little better.

During our last session together, she said, "I used to be afraid to face challenges. It felt safer to tell myself that there was nothing I could do about my problems. I worried that if I tried to make things better, I might fail. And if I failed, I'd feel even worse."

She also realized that it took a fair amount of vulnerability to share good news with friends. She was afraid someone might laugh at her if she said she might apply for a promotion or that she was going to pick up a new hobby. It had felt more comfortable to share bad news. But by the end of her treatment, she was able to be vulnerable, share good news, and gain healthy emotional support when she was struggling.

Mental Strength Exercises

To stop feeling sorry for yourself, you have to change the thoughts and actions that fuel self-pity. Here are some mental strength exercises that can help you break free from that cycle.

Turn BLUE Thoughts into True Thoughts

The thoughts that run through your head aren't always facts. Your brain lies to you. It will fill your head with irrational, unhelpful, and overly negative ideas. Fortunately, you don't have to believe everything you think. You can't stop BLUE thoughts from happening. But you can choose to respond to them with more realistic statements. So the next time you catch yourself falling into the self-pity trap, respond to those thoughts with healthier statements.

A great way to recognize unhelpful thoughts that fuel self-pity is by using the acronym BLUE. BLUE thoughts are just too negative to be true. When you catch yourself thinking BLUE thoughts, respond to them with true thoughts. BLUE stands for:

 *Blaming everyone*—While it's OK to place responsibility on others for their share of the problems, not accepting responsibility for your share paints you as a victim.

Looking for the bad news—If nine good things and one bad thing happens over the course of the day, focusing on the one bad thing can fuel self-pity.

Unhappy guessing—Predicting awful outcomes and worst-case scenarios wastes time and prevents you from taking positive action.

Exaggerating—Exaggerating how disastrous something is will cause you to feel worse.

When you feel self-pity, your brain will tell you lies that fuel even more self-pity. And that can keep you stuck. One way to break that cycle is by changing the way you think—respond to BLUE thoughts with true thoughts.

TYPE OF THOUGHT	BLUE THOUGHT	TRUE THOUGHT
Blaming everyone	No one ever does their share of the work around here.	There will be days when some people do less than others.
Looking for bad news	The concert was terrible! We had to wait in line forever.	The long line was worth the wait. The music was great.
Unhappy guessing	I'll never get out of debt.	I can create a plan to dig myself out of debt.
Exaggerating	Everyone hated my presentation today.	Some people may have found my presentation helpful.

Now take a minute to review these examples of BLUE thoughts and create a true thought you could respond with.

TYPE OF THOUGHT	BLUE THOUGHT	TRUE THOUGHT
Blaming everyone	No one on the team does anything.	
Looking for bad news	I messed up one of the interview questions.	
Unhappy guessing	No one is ever going to hire me.	
Exaggerating	I completely embarrassed myself on a first date.	

What is a recent BLUE thought you've had?

_____

_____

_____

_____

_____

What's a true thought you could respond with?

_____

_____

_____

_____

_____

Practice Radical Acceptance

I spent my first college internship working as a social worker in the dialysis unit of a hospital. Dialysis is for individuals with kidney failure. Since their kidneys can no longer filter waste products from their blood, they must filter their blood with a machine for three to five hours three days per week.

My job involved helping patients get transportation to their appointments, securing disability if they could no longer work, helping people access resources that would help them stay as healthy as possible, and providing emotional support.

Some of the patients never missed their dialysis appointments. Those who attended each session like clockwork brought things to do during their appointment. They would sit in their recliners and knit, watch movies, or read books.

Other patients, however, missed a lot of appointments. Some of them were in denial about needing dialysis. They skipped several appointments in a row and would become very ill. Others skipped appointments whenever other activities got in their way—like an opportunity to visit with friends or a chance to work overtime. The patients who weren't compliant with their treatment often faced life-threatening complications.

The difference between those who were compliant and those who weren't was their willingness to accept the illness and the lifesaving treatment they had to undergo. Of course, it's not easy to go to the hospital three days a week. But the people who treated it like a job, were quite successful at it. They accepted that this is what they had to do to stay healthy. While they didn't like going to dialysis, they accepted that for now, it was the best treatment option for them. Radical acceptance helped them live their best lives.

But you can't practice radical acceptance when you're drowning in self-pity. Feeling sorry for yourself might stem from your frustration over the unfairness of the situation you face. After all, it might not feel fair that bad things happen to good people like you. Or it might not feel fair that you've had more than your share of challenges.

But trying to resist reality wastes precious time and energy. That's why radical acceptance can help. It's an exercise in accepting things for what they are right now, fair or not.

That's not to say you can't take action. If a doctor gives you a diagnosis you don't agree with, you can accept that the doctor believes the diagnosis to be true while still seeking out a second opinion.

Radical acceptance removes judgments and sticks to the facts. It prevents us from resisting the truth.

Here are some examples of how you might respond to a resistance thought with radical acceptance. Try to fill in the blank boxes on your own.

RESISTANCE THOUGHT	RADICAL ACCEPTANCE
Why do I always have to get stuck in traffic jams? People should pay attention to where they're going and keep up with the speed limit so they don't make the rest of us sit in bumper-to-bumper traffic forever.	There are millions of cars on the road every day. Traffic jams are bound to happen sometimes.
It's not fair that my mother has one health problem after another. She can't catch a break. None of these tests ever finds anything wrong with her, and doctors don't help.	My mom is undergoing another test to see if we can find out what is happening with her health.
We deserved raises this year! The company needs to pay us more and it's not fair they aren't giving everyone more money.	
My brother shouldn't be jumping into this relationship right now. He needs to focus on himself and get things together.	

Has there been a time when you practiced radical acceptance?

_____

_____

_____

_____

_____

What's something going on in your life right now that you struggle to accept?

_____

_____

_____

_____

_____

What are some resistance thoughts you have about that situation?

_____

_____

_____

_____

_____

What's something you could tell yourself to start accepting the situation for what it is?

_____

_____

_____

_____

_____

Incorporate More Gratitude into Your Life

> *I stopped feeling sorry for myself by focusing on gratitude.*
>
> —Deborah Gish (59, Missouri)

In addition to warding off self-pity, studies show gratitude increases happiness, improves physical and mental health, and can help you sleep better. Grateful people even tend to live longer. There are many different ways to incorporate more gratitude in your life. It only takes a few minutes of your time and it doesn't cost anything. But it can have huge benefits.

Here are a few ideas for ways in which you can practice gratitude every day:

 Write in a gratitude journal—Write about three things you're grateful for each day.

 Create a gratitude jar—Write something you're grateful for every day on a slip of paper and put it in a jar. At the end of the year, read all the slips of paper to remind yourself of all the good things going on in your life.

 Create a gratitude bulletin board—Write about things you're grateful for on pieces of paper and pin them to your bulletin board.

 Establish a gratitude ritual—A daily ritual, like going around the dinner table to say what you're thankful for or texting your partner at lunch to say why you're grateful, can help you make gratitude part of your daily life.

What can you start doing right now to incorporate more gratitude into your life?

_____

_____

_____

_____

_____

Experience Gratitude

Self-pity is about thinking, "I deserve better." Gratitude is about thinking, "I have more than I deserve."

But sometimes gratitude can feel a bit like a chore rather than genuine thankfulness—like when you're writing a stack of thank-you notes. So while it can be helpful to incorporate gratitude practices into your daily routine, you may want to shift your thinking a little if your gratitude practices seem to be getting somewhat stale.

Here's a helpful strategy for experiencing true gratitude: rather than thinking about how thankful you are that someone bought you a present or spent time helping you with something, think about how you feel about that person. Imagine that person shopping for that gift for you. How does it feel to know that person spent their time really looking for a gift they thought you'd enjoy? Or how does it feel to think that someone took time out of their day to help you with something?

Thinking about gratitude in those terms can conjure up true thankfulness for the people in your life.

What's a time when someone in your life did something kind for you or gave you something?

_____

_____

_____

_____

_____

What emotions do you feel when you think about that person doing that for you?

_____

_____

_____

_____

_____

What are some things you'd like to say to that person about how you feel about them?

_____

_____

_____

_____

_____

Do Something That Makes Self-Pity Nearly Impossible

Staying in bed, isolating yourself from people, and complaining are just a few behaviors that fuel self-pity. Fortunately, there are steps you can take that make it much harder to feel sorry for yourself.

You may have to push yourself to do things you don't want to do, like meet up with a friend to talk about pleasant subjects. But it's important to challenge yourself to go do something that can help you break free.

What can you do when you catch yourself feeling sorry for yourself?

☐ Do something kind for someone else

☐ Visit a friend or family member

☐ Share positive things on social media

☐ Do something on your to-do list

☐ Volunteer to help others

☐ Exercise

☐ Read a book

☐ _____

Prevent Self-Pity

There may be times in your life when you can predict that you're likely to feel sorry for yourself. Maybe you always struggle with self-pity as the holidays draw closer. Or maybe you feel sorry for yourself when winter rolls around and you can't do a lot of the activities you enjoy. In those cases, preventative measures can help you stop self-pity in your tracks.

In *13 Things Mentally Strong People Don't Do*, I share an example of how I do this in my own life. On my late husband's birthday, his family and I go on an adventure every year. Our adventures include things like skydiving, swimming with sharks, zip-lining, riding mules into the Grand Canyon, surfing, and even taking flying-trapeze lessons. Whatever the adventure is, getting together and doing something out of the ordinary has been a great way to ward off self-pity on a difficult day.

If there's a date or a time of year that makes it easy for you to feel sorry for yourself, find a way to prevent yourself from falling into the self-pity trap. You don't necessarily have to jump out of a plane. Anything from scheduling dinner with friends to volunteering to help a good cause might help you feel better.

What's a time in the future when you might be tempted to feel sorry for yourself?

_____

_____

_____

_____

_____

What can you do to prevent self-pity?

_____

_____

_____

_____

_____

Express genuine gratitude toward a different person each day this week. Call your grandmother to say how much you appreciate that she read stories with you as a kid, have coffee with a friend who has made a difference in your life and tell them how grateful you are, or tell a family member how thankful you are that they have helped you during tough times in your life.

Create Your Plan to Stop Feeling Sorry for Yourself

What are some things you can do to allow yourself to feel bad without slipping into self-pity?

- ☐ Reach for healthy coping skills when I feel sad
- ☐ Reframe unhelpful thoughts that fuel feelings of self-pity
- ☐ Refuse to invite other people to attend my pity parties
- ☐ Take action that makes self-pity impossible
- ☐ Resist the urge to complain in an effort to gain sympathy
- ☐ Practice radical acceptance
- ☐ Incorporate gratitude rituals into my day
- ☐ _____

Now let's identify some clear action steps you can start taking right away. Some steps might be meant to help you ward off self-pity and others might be strategies you can employ if you start feeling sorry for yourself. Here are some examples:

- When someone turns down my invitation to do something fun, I'll invite someone else.

- When I get rejected for something, I'll commit to trying again.

- When someone does something unkind to me, I'll do something kind for someone else.

- When someone declines a favor, I'll ask someone else for help.

- When I feel helpless, I will find something to do to help someone else.

- When I start thinking my life won't get any better, I'll volunteer or do something to help make the world a better place.

What's one step you can take to stop wasting time feeling sorry for yourself?

_____
_____
_____
_____
_____
_____

What will you notice about yourself once you stop wasting time feeling sorry for yourself?

_____
_____
_____
_____
_____
_____

How will your life be different?

_____

_____

_____

_____

_____

_____

When I **STOPPED** giving away my power . . .

I felt invigorated and empowered realizing that there are a lot of things I am actually in charge of and can make a positive change for my job.

—Tess Naaijkens (48, Spain)

I realized how powerful I am. It's energizing to see just how much I can do when I reserve that power for myself.

—Nikki Walker, (43, Nevada)

I stopped believing everyone else's opinions of me and started listening to myself.

—Kenny Austin (31, New Jersey)

Don't
Give Away
Your Power

OUT OF ALL of the 13 Things, "don't give away your power" resonates with readers most. I frequently receive messages that say things like, "I never realized I was giving so many other people power over my life." These messages come from people from all walks of life.

I once gave a keynote in Washington, DC, to a room filled with high-powered officials who were appointed by the president. After my talk, a tall man dressed in a sharp suit walked up to me and said, "I've been giving away my power to my mother-in-law for a long time. I want to change that." Clearly, no matter how powerful you might be in one area of your life, you might still give away your power in another area.

You can't create the best life for yourself until you take complete responsibility for your thoughts, feelings, and actions. But before you can do that, you have to stop giving other people that power.

How Do You Give Away Your Power?

In this chapter, we'll discuss some subtle (and not-so-subtle) ways you might be giving away your power and the steps you can take to empower yourself. Before we do, take a minute to look over the following list and place a checkmark next to the statements that sound like you.

- ☐ I give other people the power to evoke reactions from me that I don't like, such as raising my voice.
- ☐ I give other people the power to ruin my day.
- ☐ Praise and criticism have a huge impact on how I think about myself.
- ☐ I change my behavior based on who is around me.
- ☐ I blame people for wasting my time.
- ☐ I feel obligated to accept invitations.
- ☐ I blame people for taking advantage of me.

☐ I'm only OK if the people around me are doing OK.

☐ My mind is often preoccupied with thoughts about people I don't like.

☐ I spend a lot of time rehashing unpleasant situations or dreading things I don't want to do.

☐ I often blame other people for *making* me feel a certain way.

You might find you only give away your power to certain people or during specific circumstances. Or you might find that you give away your power every day. Either way, there are steps you can take to empower yourself and regain your mental strength.

What are some specific ways in which you might be giving away your power? Don't worry if you aren't quite sure yet. Just give it your best here.

_____

_____

_____

_____

_____

Coming up next, we'll get into more details about how to identify the exact ways in which you might be giving away your power.

Giving Away Your Power vs. Empowering Yourself

There are many ways in which you might give someone power over your thoughts, feelings, and behavior.

Sometimes it involves being around people physically—like attending a family event you don't want to go to only because you want to avoid your mother's guilt trip. In this case, you give your mother power over your behavior.

> People who care so little for me definitely shouldn't control any of my thoughts or emotions.
>
> —Dave (59, Michigan)

At other times, you might give power to someone even when you don't see them physically. For example, let's say someone hurt you a decade ago. You might still spend a lot of time thinking about that person, which allows them to occupy a huge space in your life. You give that person power over your thoughts and your time.

You might also give someone power over your feelings. If someone says something you don't like and you spend the entire day feeling angry, you give that person power over your emotional state.

There isn't a one-size-fits-all answer about how to empower yourself. In some cases, it might involve speaking up to someone whose behavior you don't appreciate. But there may be times when empowering yourself involves walking away from a conversation so you don't waste your time and energy getting into a heated argument.

Empowering yourself might involve saying no to some things you don't want to do. There may be plenty of times, however, that you choose to do things that you aren't excited about—like helping a friend move—because that's part of being a good friend. It's all about your ability to recognize that what you're doing is your choice.

GIVING AWAY YOUR POWER	EMPOWERING YOURSELF
Holding a grudge	Choosing to let go of anger
Walking on eggshells around someone	Letting someone be responsible for their feelings
Waiting on someone to take action	Taking action by yourself
Giving in to someone out of guilt	Sticking to no

Who Are You Giving Your Power To?

To help you get started in figuring out who you give your power to, answer the following questions:

Who do you dread seeing?	
What do you think about often even though you don't want to?	
Who brings out the worst in you?	
Who do you lose your temper with?	
Who do you blame for wasting your time?	

Which patterns do you notice about the above names? Do you give away your power mostly to friends? Family members? Colleagues? Do you see the same name popping up over and over?

_____

_____

_____

_____

_____

How Are You Giving Away Your Power?

Now that you've started thinking about *who* you give your power to, let's talk about the *ways* in which you might allow people to have a negative influence on the way you think, feel, and behave.

In certain cases, someone might mostly affect the way you think. You might waste four hours of your life rehashing something they said. There may also be times when you experience a lot of anxiety when you're with someone, meaning you give them power over how you feel. And at other times, you might give someone power over your behavior by giving in to unhealthy choices when you're with them.

Of course, there will be instances when your thoughts, behaviors, and feelings are all affected. The more you think about something, the worse you might feel. And those feelings will likely impact the actions you take (or don't take).

It's important to recognize the different ways in which your thoughts, feelings, and behaviors might change when you give someone too much power in your life.

What are the specific things you do to give away your power?

☐ I think about someone more than I want to.

☐ I allow someone to drag down my mood.

☐ I let someone occupy more of my time than I want them to.

☐ I allow someone's criticism to change how I feel about myself.

☐ I allow someone to treat me poorly.

☐ I let someone have a negative influence on my habits (e.g., spending too much money or drinking more than I want).

☐ _____

☐ _____

What's an example of a time when you gave someone power over your thoughts?

_____

_____

_____

_____

_____

What's an example of a time when you gave someone power over your emotions?

_____

_____

_____

_____

_____

What's an example of a time when you gave someone power over your behavior?

_____

_____

_____

_____

_____

Why You Give Away Your Power

You won't change your behavior until you recognize why you're doing it. There are many reasons why you might give someone power over your life. To help you figure out what's at the root of giving away your power, see how many of these statements sound like you.

☐ I am afraid of upsetting someone.

☐ I don't really know who I am, so I believe what other people say about me.

☐ I judge myself based on how other people feel about me.

☐ I don't know how to speak up for myself.

☐ I feel anxious about setting boundaries or telling someone no.

☐ I am afraid people might leave me if I do what's best for me.

☐ I don't want to appear selfish.

☐ I am afraid of hurting someone's feelings.

☐ I pick up on the emotions of everyone around me.

☐ I hate confrontation.

☐ _____

Giving away your power often starts small. You may give someone just a hint of power over your life one day. But you keep giving them a little more each day until they have a lot of power over the way you think, feel, and behave.

> This taught me to not give away my power such that no one can ruin my day or my emotions. My happiness depends on me and me alone.
>
> —Nancy Katana (40, Kenya)

Sometimes we give away our power to people we don't like. At other times, however, we give away power to people we really love.

That was the case with my client Brian. Brian was much more reserved than his passionate girlfriend. He felt confused when she raised her voice, stormed off, or occasionally threatened to end the relationship.

Whenever he said something she didn't like, she would leave. On the way out the door, she'd yell something like, "You'll appreciate me someday!"

As soon as she'd slam the door, Brian's anxiety skyrocketed. He'd spend the next several hours texting her incessantly. He'd apologize (even though most of the time he had no idea what he had done wrong), beg her to come home, and ask her to reassure him that they hadn't broken up.

She usually ignored him for hours and then would reply with vague messages that kept him on edge like, "I can't answer the phone right now. I'm busy hanging out with people who actually care about me." Replies like that fueled Brian's anxiety and he'd spend the entire night obsessively checking her social media accounts and texting her to come home. If he happened to have plans, he'd cancel them because he wanted to make sure he was home if she decided to return.

After a few nights like that, Brian began to walk on eggshells. He spent much of his time trying to avoid upsetting his girlfriend (even though he could never really figure out what would set her off).

When she seemed upset, he couldn't function. He'd waste endless hours trying to calm her down and convince her to come home.

Through several therapy sessions, Brian was able to recognize why he gave his girlfriend so much power. He was terrified she was going to leave him. He had a deep-down fear that he wasn't good enough and his self-worth depended on his girlfriend sticking with him. He felt powerless when she threatened to leave him. Understanding why he gave her so much power was the first step toward taking the action that would heal him.

He also began learning how to set healthy boundaries. Sometimes that meant speaking up, and at other times it meant walking away from behavior that he didn't want to engage in. He worked on finding healthy strategies to cope with his anxiety so he wouldn't send multiple messages to his girlfriend when she wasn't responding.

He discovered that changing his behavior changed their relationship. In therapy, we like to say a relationship is like a dance. When you change your steps, your partner will change their steps too.

As things changed in the relationship, Brian came to the conclusion that he and his girlfriend likely weren't compatible over the long term. But empowering himself helped him feel confident in his ability to tolerate ending a relationship he began to view as unhealthy, and he broke up with his girlfriend—something he once never imagined himself being able to do. By the end of treatment, he believed in himself and he had hope that he could find a healthier relationship with someone who felt empowered as well.

Mental Strength Exercises

When you start focusing on strategies that empower you, you'll be less likely to give away your power to other people. Here are some of my favorite mental strength exercises that can help you stop giving away your power.

Change Your Language

Your words are powerful. They can either imply you're a victim or they can empower you to take control over your life. It's not just the words you say out loud—the words you use inside your own head matter too.

It's common to use language that implies someone is taking your power. That's victim language. Choose different words to show that you are in control of how you think, how you feel, how you act, how you spend your time, and who you spend it with. Fill in the blank boxes with empowered language.

VICTIM MENTALITY	EMPOWERED MENTALITY
My coworker wastes my time talking about her personal life.	I can end a conversation whenever I want.
My sister makes me feel self-conscious.	I am in charge of how I feel about myself.
I have to loan my brother money so he doesn't get evicted.	I choose whether to loan my brother money.
I always have to work late.	
My mother-in-law ruins our peaceful weekends.	

What are some examples of phrases you use that give away your power?

_____

_____

_____

_____

_____

Which phrases can you use to empower yourself?

_____

_____

_____

_____

_____

Chart Your Time

Time is your most valuable resource. You can always make more money but you can't create more time. Once it's gone, it's gone.

That's why it's so important to invest your time wisely. And one of the easiest ways to give away your power is by giving away your time to people or circumstances who aren't worthy of this precious resource.

> *I wake up and remind myself that whatever I do today is my choice. It empowers me to take control over how I spend my time and prevents me from blaming other people for "wasting it" or "stealing it."*
>
> —Cory S. (33, New York)

Sometimes it's helpful to see where all your time is going. Seeing your time mapped out can help you recognize people or circumstances you are giving more time to than you want. Once you're aware of this, you can take steps to take back your power by being proactive about where you invest your time.

This is an exercise I did with my therapy client Amber. She thought she never had enough time to get things done. She spent much of her life feeling worn out and run-down.

Our work together involved looking at all the ways in which she was giving away her power—and who she was giving it to. With a little help, she was able to see that people weren't taking her power. She was giving it to them.

Together, we created this list of the people she was giving her power to and how she was giving it away. Here's what she found:

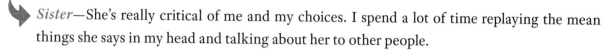 *Sister*—She's really critical of me and my choices. I spend a lot of time replaying the mean things she says in my head and talking about her to other people.

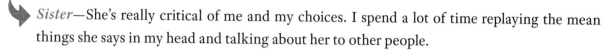 *Ex-boyfriend*—We broke up a few months ago and haven't had much contact. I check out his social media accounts almost every day. And I look to see what his friends and family members are doing on social media too because I want more information about whether he's dating yet.

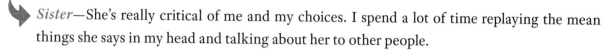 *Boss*—My boss often assigns extra projects to me. I never speak up and tell her that I don't have time and I never ask for help. I think she's unreasonable and I spend a lot of time complaining about how much I don't like my job.

Those were three people she was allowing to have a negative influence on her life. She wanted to give them the least amount of her time and attention, yet she realized she was devoting more energy to them than the people whose company she actually enjoyed. To see exactly how much time and energy she was giving them, we created a pie chart that broke down how she'd spent the previous day.

Actual Time

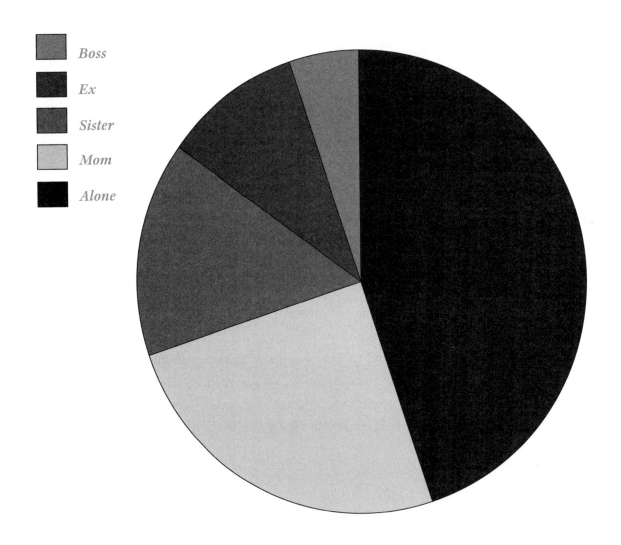

Boss
Ex
Sister
Mom
Alone

She had spent some time talking to her mom, which she really liked, and she spent a lot of time by herself, which she thoroughly enjoyed. But she realized that even though she didn't physically see her sister, her ex, or her boss the previous day (it was Sunday), they still occupied a lot of her mental energy. She talked about them and thought about them way more than she wanted to.

So we created a more ideal time line based on how she'd actually like to spend her time and energy. She still wanted to spend a fair amount of time alone and she wanted to increase the amount of time she focused on her mom (that meant spending quality time with her without complaining about or talking about the people she was giving her power to). She also realized she wanted her friends to occupy more space in her life and she thought her time would be better spent playing with her cat rather than perseverating on what her ex was doing.

Ideal Time

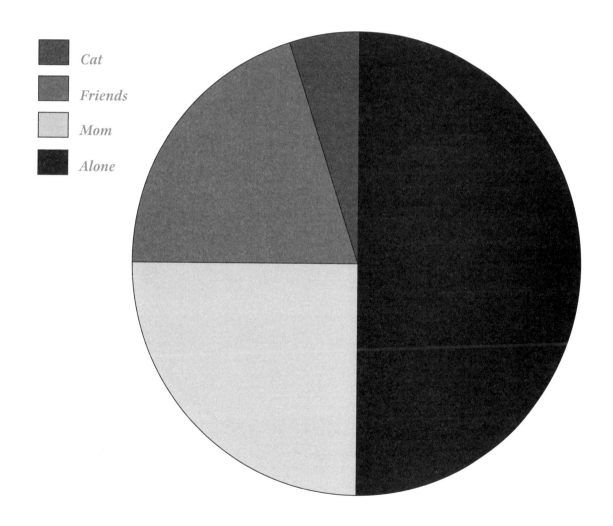

Seeing the difference between the pie charts reinforced her decision to create some changes in her life. She started checking in with herself about how she was spending her time every day. Whenever she was tempted to complain about her sister or check her ex's social media, she reminded herself what her ideal day looked like.

You might find that a visual helps you too. Use the following circle to identify who actually gets your time and energy. Fill it in to depict the people who are getting the bulk of your time and mental energy. Keep in mind that these may not be the same people you physically spend time with. They might be the people who you think about or talk about.

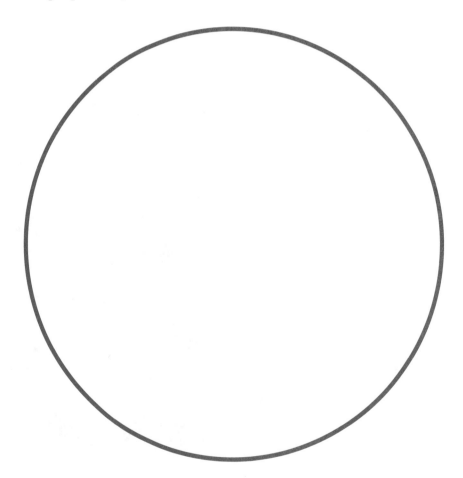

Now, use this pie chart to create your ideal day. If you were to get proactive about who gets your time and mental energy, how would you divide it up?

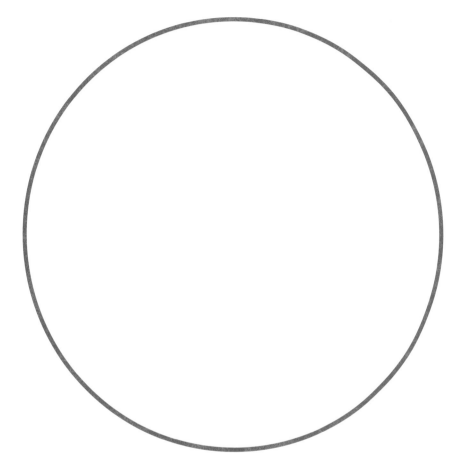

Now that you've seen the differences between the two circles, you may have a visual representation of the people who are taking up more space in your life than you'd like. Who are you giving away your power to right now and what steps do you want to take to change that?

_____

_____

_____

_____

_____

Create Boundaries

When you blame someone for stealing your time or taking advantage of your kindness, it's a sure-fire sign that you need to create better boundaries in your life. You might need to decline social invitations, end conversations, or stop answering the phone.

Boundaries are the lines you draw that outline your expectations of how you want to be treated. Some boundaries are created with words; others with your behavior.

You might tell your mother-in-law that you would like her to call first instead of showing up at your house unannounced. Explaining that boundary ahead of time makes your expectations clear.

Boundaries don't always need to be announced out loud. You might choose to leave a family gathering whenever people start drinking. You don't necessarily need to warn everyone ahead of time or make a big deal out of the fact that you're leaving. Instead, your feet will communicate for you as you walk away.

What are some examples of boundaries you've already set with people in your life?

_____

_____

_____

_____

_____

What are some new boundaries you could create to empower yourself?

_____

_____

_____

_____

_____

This Week's Homework

Keep track of anyone you're tempted to give your power to this week. Write down who the individual was and the circumstance. By the end of the week you'll discover some patterns—like if you give power to your family, or if you give away your power when you're feeling anxious.

Create Your Plan to Empower Yourself

What are some things you can do to start empowering yourself?

☐ Say no to things I don't want to do

☐ Speak up when I don't like the way I'm being treated

☐ Invest more time/energy into my own activities

☐ Practice taking care of myself better

☐ Distract myself when I'm ruminating on someone or a situation

☐ Change victim language to empowered language

☐ Regulate my emotions

☐ Forgive someone

☐ _____

Now let's identify some clear action steps you can take. Remember, small steps can go a long way when taken consistently. Here are some examples of small steps you might take.

➤ I'll excuse myself the next time my coworkers are gossiping in the break room so I don't get caught up in it with them.

➤ I won't pick up the phone when I'm eating dinner.

➤ When I feel myself getting upset in a conversation, I'll say I need to take a break to calm down before I lose my temper.

➤ When I'm anxious about whether my partner is upset with me, I'll go to the gym rather than text them repeatedly.

➤ When I find myself rehashing conversations I had with my boss that didn't go well, I'll talk to my partner about something unrelated to work.

➤ The next time my brother asks me to borrow money, I'll say no.

➤ I'll practice working on forgiving my mother for not being able to show me a lot of love as a child.

➤ When I catch myself using victim language I will replace it with language that empowers me.

What's one step you can take to start taking back your power?

_____

_____

_____

_____

_____

_____

What will you notice about yourself once you start taking back your power?

_____

_____

_____

_____

_____

_____

How will your life be different when you stop giving away your power?

_____

_____

_____

_____

_____

_____

When I **STOPPED** shying away from change . . .

I realized just how much I have been missing and just how much more I am capable of.

— Brian McDonald (38, Canada)

I started a new job, moved to a better house, and made new friends. It was hard in the short term, but was worth it in the long term!

— Sarah Thomas (37, Oregon)

I discovered how beautiful I could make my life.

— Megan Gordon (26, New Mexico)

Don't
Shy Away
from Change

MY CLIENTS OFTEN tell me, "But I hate change!" My job isn't to make them love change. Change is hard. But avoiding change won't do you any good.

During the COVID-19 pandemic, we saw just how quickly our circumstances can change. Whether you had to wear a mask, work from home, miss out on social events, or suspend your vacation, you had to adapt. Some people discovered they wanted even more change—they switched jobs, moved to a new place, or adopted some healthy new habits.

Other people couldn't wait for things to return to some sense of "normal" so they could get back into their old routine. But if the pandemic taught us anything, it's that sometimes the whole world can change pretty fast.

There's nothing wrong with enjoying a simple life or choosing to be content with the way things are. It's also OK to have regular routines and healthy habits that are set to autopilot. But it's important to be adaptable so that when things around you change, you can grow alongside it.

How Do You Shy Away from Change?

In this chapter, we'll discuss how to find the courage to create positive changes in your life. Before we dive in, take a look at the following statements and place a checkmark next to the ones that sound like you.

☐ I stay in a job/relationship/situation that I know isn't good for me.

☐ I often think about how changes could make things worse, not better.

☐ When I try something new, I'm quick to give up because it feels uncomfortable.

☐ I pass up opportunities because I don't want to do something new.

☐ I've stayed in a relationship (friendship or romantic) that wasn't good for me because it felt familiar.

☐ When other people change something that affects me, I am quick to protest.

What's an example of a time when you shied away from change?

_____

_____

_____

_____

_____

What were you thinking at the time?

_____

_____

_____

_____

What were you feeling?

_____

_____

_____

_____

Changing on the Inside vs. Changing on the Outside

Some people are too quick to adopt change. They change jobs, relationships, and living situations at the first hint that the grass is greener on the other side.

While they are changing their environment, they aren't changing themselves. They might be uncomfortable with boredom. Or they might not know what they want from life or even who they really are. Or, they might just be running from their problems.

On the other hand, there may be areas of your life in which you're really slow to change. Perhaps you've stayed in the same unhealthy relationship far too long because you are afraid of being lonely. Or maybe you've stayed at a job you didn't like because you thought finding a new job would take too much effort.

What's an example of a time when you've been too quick to change something on the outside because you really didn't want to change on the inside?

_____

_____

_____

_____

_____

What's a change you've resisted making because it felt too uncomfortable or it felt like too much work?

_____

_____

_____

_____

_____

Why Do You Shy Away from Change?

We often opt for familiarity over uncertainty, even though taking a chance might make things better. Even when things are bad, we like it when life is predictable. But there are other reasons why you might avoid change in your life. Take a few minutes to review the following statements and decide which ones sound true to you.

☐ I say no to new opportunities out of habit.

☐ I think of all the things that could go wrong if I do something differently.

☐ I doubt my ability to adapt to something new.

☐ Doing something new causes me to feel anxiety and I'll do just about anything not to be anxious.

☐ Change just feels too hard.

☐ I am afraid one small change could cause everything to fall apart.

☐ I think doing things differently requires more effort than I can give.

☐ I halfheartedly try something new and at the first sign of a problem, I bail.

☐ When I try something new, I spend my energy thinking about how things were better before rather than focusing on adapting.

☐ _____

Lindsey hadn't felt well for several months but her symptoms varied. One day she'd have a debilitating headache, the next day she would be doubled over with a stomachache. Her husband and her parents insisted she see her doctor, as her fatigue and pain issues didn't seem normal.

But the more they pushed, the more she resisted. She did, however, agree to see a therapist. That's how she landed in my therapy office.

She said, "I already know what a doctor is going to tell me—I need to lose weight, get more exercise, and eat healthier. But how can I do those things when I'm so stressed-out all the time?"

She knew her family meant well by insisting she get help. But she felt certain they didn't understand she couldn't possibly change her habits until she felt better emotionally.

So we spent several weeks talking about the things that caused her stress and how she handled it. She acknowledged that she spent a lot of time eating unhealthy food, watching TV, and staying in bed. She was hopeful that talk therapy could relieve her stress so she'd have the energy to create positive changes.

So while it was true that reducing her stress would likely help her create positive changes, I explained that the reverse was also likely true. Creating positive changes in her life would likely reduce her stress.

Part of her treatment involved tackling her belief that she had to feel better first so she could make positive changes later. She began reminding herself that she could make some changes now even though she didn't feel up to it.

She agreed to start by making an appointment with her physician to rule out any serious health problems. And just as she suspected, her doctor advised her to develop some healthier habits.

She came into therapy after that appointment saying, "I already don't feel well. I'm afraid pushing myself to do things is going to make me feel even worse."

Even though Lindsey's quality of life wasn't very high at that moment, she feared any step she might take might reduce her quality of life even more So we worked on a strategy called "Play to Win," an exercise we'll cover later in this chapter. Essentially, it involved shifting her thoughts from "I hope getting more physical activity doesn't make my life worse" to "I hope getting more physical activity makes my life better." That subtle change made a big difference.

She started paying attention to the ways in which change could be good for her. Of course, there were no guarantees that healthier habits were going to help her feel physically and emotionally better. But we wouldn't know unless she tried.

But once her mantra became "I'm going to make my life better," not "I'm going to avoid making my life worse," she found the courage to try some new things. She started small. She went for a walk around the block before work and then again after dinner. And she wrote down what she was eating every day.

Within a week she said just those little changes helped her feel a little better. So we started identifying a few more little changes she could implement—like doing some stretching and drinking more water. With each change she made, she gained confidence in her ability to do things differently.

By the end of our time together, Lindsey felt empowered. She took charge of her health and her well-being. And she acknowledged that her stress level declined once she started creating better habits for herself. She trusted that she could not only tolerate change, but she could also create it.

> *I started saying yes to things. I realized qualities in me I never knew I had. I met people and formed relationships that now are friendships. I even have a job I love because I took that leap of faith and stepped out of the boat. I got out of my comfort zone and found these new experiences and relationships were what was missing in my life. Had I shied away, which everything in me wanted to do, I wouldn't have found myself. Whether the experience was one I stuck with or one I tried and didn't like, at least now I had the peace of mind of knowing.*
>
> —Jenny Dickerson (39, Michigan)

Mental Strength Exercises

To stop shying away from change you need confidence that you can adapt. Sometimes, a few little changes to the way you think or the way you act can make a big difference in your willingness to tackle a change head-on. Here are some of my favorite exercises that can help you build the mental strength you need to stop shying away from change.

Name Your Emotions

Just putting a label on how you're feeling can take a lot of the sting out of your emotions. Naming a feeling helps your brain make a little more sense of what's going on in your body. So when you can say, "I'm anxious right now," or "I'm sad," that emotion might feel a little less intense.

When you shy away from change, it's likely because you're trying to avoid an uncomfortable emotion. It might feel scary to try something new. Or it might feel sad to end something that isn't working. Acknowledging that uncomfortable emotion you're trying to avoid might give you the courage you need to face it.

Don't be alarmed if you struggle to find a word that describes how you feel. We rarely talk about emotions so it can be tough to know how you're feeling. Here's a simple list of feeling words that can get you started:

Happy	Sad	Mad	Lonely
Anxious	Surprised	Jealous	Scared
Embarrassed	Disgusted	Frustrated	Confident
Confused	Grateful	Playful	Guilty
Disappointed	Shocked	Overwhelmed	Peaceful

What's a change you're avoiding in your life right now?

_____

_____

_____

_____

What's the uncomfortable emotion(s) you're trying to avoid feeling?

_____

_____

_____

_____

Play to Win

You might be avoiding a change because you are afraid of making things worse. But trying to avoid making things worse is much different than trying to crush your goal.

If you arrive at the first day of your new job thinking, "I hope I don't hate this job as much as I did my last job," you'll likely have a much different experience than if you walk in thinking, "I hope I love my job!'

I guarantee an Olympic athlete doesn't step onto the court or the field thinking, "I hope I don't come in last." They're there to win! And it's their "play to win" attitude that helps them become elite athletes.

Approach change the same way. Decide that you're going to make your life better with the changes you make. Check out the following examples of how you might think when you're trying not to lose versus how you might think when you're trying to win. Then see if you can fill in the blank boxes with your own examples of how you could change your thoughts so you're playing to win.

TRYING NOT TO LOSE	TRYING TO WIN
I hope this date isn't awful.	I hope this date is a lot of fun.
I'm going to embarrass myself in Spin class.	I'm going to meet new people and get in a good workout.
I don't want to have the fewest sales in my division.	
I hope my friends don't laugh at my outfit.	
I don't want to get fired at my annual review.	
I hope I don't burn dinner.	

What's an example of a situation where you are playing to avoid losing?

_____

_____

_____

_____

_____

What are some of the thoughts you have about that situation?

_____

_____

_____

_____

_____

How can you change that thought so that you're playing to win?

_____

_____

_____

_____

_____

Argue the Opposite

Your brain might be really good at predicting worst-case scenarios. It might also be really good at staying focused on how a bad outcome is imminent.

If someone told you that you had a one in a million chance of winning a raffle you just entered, you'd probably walk away knowing you weren't going to win. You might not even spend another minute thinking about it.

But if you have a one in a million chance of contracting a deadly disease, you might find your-

> _I had to start looking at all the reasons I was working so hard to keep everything the same. I was lying to myself about how hard change was going to be. When I stopped thinking about all the things that could go wrong and started thinking about all the things that might go right, I found the courage I need to change my life._
>
> —Carolyn Highwater (47, Minnesota)

self convinced that you're going to get it. You might waste countless hours perseverating on the fact that you're at risk.

That's often how our brains respond to change. We overestimate the potential risks while also underestimating our ability to handle the outcome.

One thing you can do to combat those negative thoughts is to argue the opposite. Take a minute and try to come up with the best-case scenario. Think about how things might go even better than you might expect. Fill in the blank boxes with your own examples of how you could argue the opposite.

UNHELPFUL THOUGHT	ARGUE THE OPPOSITE
Everyone is going to hate my presentation.	Everyone might like my presentation.
This event is going to be awkward.	This event is going to be really fun.
The doctor is going to give me bad news.	
No one is going to show up.	
My relationship is never going to get any better.	
I'll never be able to get healthier.	
I am always going to be broke.	

What's a worst-case scenario you're imagining right now?

_____

_____

_____

_____

_____

What's the potential best-case scenario?

_____

_____

_____

_____

_____

Use the STEPS to Problem-Solving

Sometimes, we stay right where we are because there are obstacles in our path and we aren't sure how to overcome them. At other times, we feel so overwhelmed by life that we can't muster the energy to do anything differently.

You might convince yourself that there are no solutions. Or you might think the only solution is just too far out of reach. But there are always multiple ways to solve the same problem and many ways to get to a solution.

> *I spent a long time convincing myself I couldn't change my life. But many of the obstacles I thought stood in my way weren't really obstacles meant to stop me. They were just challenges that required me to get creative enough to work through.*
>
> —William R. (41, France)

Having a clear problem-solving strategy can help you tackle whatever challenges you face. One strategy is to use STEPS. It's an acronym that stands for:

- Say what the problem is

- Think of at least five solutions

- Evaluate the pros and cons of each one

- Pick one

- See if it works

Here's an example:

Lucas's rent increased every year. He had thought about moving but he didn't have much money saved. Most apartments required the first and last months' rent and a security deposit in advance. So he often told himself he was going to have to live in the same building forever. Here's how he could use the STEPS to problem-solving:

- Say what the problem is—I need to save at least $5,000 so I can move.

- Think of at least five solutions

    1. I can apply for part-time jobs to earn more money

    2. I could quit paying rent at my current place

    3. I can reduce my other expenses

    4. I could sell my car

    5. I could stay with my parents for a few months

Evaluate the potential pros and cons of each idea

IDEA	PRO	CON
I can apply for part-time jobs.	I could likely get hired fast for a small job.	I won't have time to do fun things.
I could quit paying rent at my current place to save money.	I could save money in a couple of months.	My landlord will not give me a good reference; I might ruin my credit.
I can reduce my expenses to save money.	It would be good for me to review my budget.	It will take a long time to save enough money.
I could sell my car.	I could get the money fast.	I will have to pay for ride share services.
I could stay with my parents for a few months.	I could save money fast.	I don't really want to stay with them; I'd need to figure out what to do with all my stuff.

 Pick one—Find a part-time job

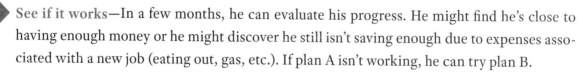 See if it works—In a few months, he can evaluate his progress. He might find he's close to having enough money or he might discover he still isn't saving enough due to expenses associated with a new job (eating out, gas, etc.). If plan A isn't working, he can try plan B.

Now take a problem in your life and work through the STEPS to problem-solving. Brainstorm as many solutions as you can—they don't all have to be things you would necessarily try. Identifying a variety of options can help you see that there are many ways to solve the same problem.

<u>Say what the problem is:</u>

_____

_____

_____

_____

_____

<u>Think of at least five solutions:</u>

_____

_____

_____

_____

_____

<u>Evaluate what is good or bad about each of the above solutions:</u>

GOOD	BAD
1.	
2.	
3.	
4.	
5.	

Pick one.

_____

_____

_____

_____

_____

See if it works. If not, what's another solution you can try?

_____

_____

_____

_____

_____

What are some other problems or issues you could apply STEPS to in your life?

_____

_____

_____

_____

_____

How might solving those problems help you embrace change?

_____

_____

_____

_____

_____

Practice naming your feelings a few times every day. You might pair this with an activity you already do so it's easier to remember—like brushing your teeth or eating a meal. Check in with yourself and ask, "How am I feeling right now?" The more you name your feelings, the easier it is to identify the emotions that may cause you to shy away from change.

Create Your Plan to Stop Shying Away from Change

What are some things you can do to stop shying away from change?

- ☐ Try one new thing every week
- ☐ Pay attention to my feelings when I'm tempted to shy away from change
- ☐ Identify the problems I'm scared to face
- ☐ Ask for help to create change when I'm struggling to do so on my own
- ☐ Identify areas of my life that are stagnant and evaluate what changes I want to make
- ☐ _____

Now let's identify some clear action steps you could take to start embracing change. Here are some examples of steps someone might take to stop shying away from change:

➤ I will sign up for a new class this week.

➤ I will spend one hour a week learning about technology.

➤ I will spend Saturday mornings researching new apartment options.

➤ I will update my résumé and apply for one new job each week.

➤ I will accept one new opportunity that comes my way each month.

What's one step you can take to start embracing change?

_____

_____

_____

_____

_____

_____

What will you notice about yourself once you start welcoming change?

_____

_____

_____

_____

_____

_____

How will your life be different?

_____

_____

_____

_____

_____

_____

When I **STOPPED** focusing on Things I Can't Control

I was able to focus on the things I could control.

—Blayne Watts (46, Montana)

I developed a better sense of trust in others and their abilities. Working in a job that operates on time lines and competing priorities, being able to trust others to accomplish tasks within range of their abilities, I have realized that it frees me up to focus on coaching and developing them, which is one of my priorities.

—Wesley Champlin (51, Florida)

I realized how much time I can put into the things I can control. That made all the difference in the world to me.

—Lanna Bailey (62, Maryland)

Don't Focus on Things You Can't Control

YOU'LL LIKELY FIND that there are times when it seems easier to control the environment than it does to control your emotions. This approach makes sense much of the time. After all, if there's an event that is going to create a lot of stress, you might wisely decide not to attend.

But there are times this strategy backfires. You might spend countless hours obsessing over things you can't actually control—you just wish you could. We all focus on things we can't control sometimes. And when we do, it wastes our valuable time and energy and introduces new problems into our lives.

It's scary to shift to focusing on things you can control—at least at first. If you're a chronic worrier you understand what I mean. The whole reason you work so hard to fix certain circumstances or change other people is because you're concerned about what will happen if you don't. But once you stop focusing on the things you can't control, you'll have a lot more time and energy to focus on the things you can control.

How Do You Focus on Things You Can't Control?

In this chapter, we'll discuss what's really within your control and what isn't and we'll work on some exercises that will help you start putting your attention where it matters most—on the things you can control. But first, let's take a look at some different ways in which you might be putting your focus on things you can't control.

☐ I obsessively research things I have no control over because I experience less anxiety as long as I am doing something.

☐ I spend a lot of time predicting catastrophic outcomes.

☐ I invest a lot of time in thinking about how other people should change.

☐ I spend a lot of time asking myself "What if . . ." questions that aren't helpful, like "What if no one shows up?"

☐ I replay things that already happened in my mind over and over again.

☐ I worry a lot about other people's problems and how they're going to handle them.

☐ I spend more time thinking about what other people are going to say or do rather than think about myself.

What is something you spend a lot of time thinking about even though you have no control over it?

_____

_____

_____

_____

_____

How do you feel when you think about that thing?

_____

_____

_____

_____

What do you do when you're thinking about it? How does it affect your behavior?

_____

_____

_____

_____

Focusing on Things You Can't Control vs. Focusing on Things You Can Control

If we could control the world, we could eliminate anxiety. But we can't prevent bad things from happening and we can't make things go our way.

That doesn't mean we don't try. Most of us invest energy in things we have zero control over at least some of the time.

Maybe you've spent countless hours worrying about how your adult child was going to spend her money. Or maybe you worried about what your boss was going to say at your next meeting.

That's not to say you shouldn't spend some time thinking about your own behavior. You might create a plan for what you'll say to a daughter who struggles to live within her means. Or you might plan for how you'll respond if your boss criticizes your work.

But there's a difference between productive thinking and ruminating on things that you can't control.

Let's say you planned a big outdoor celebration for someone this weekend. And the weather calls for a chance of rain. It's helpful to have a plan for what you'll do if it rains. It's not helpful to obsessively check multiple weather apps every few minutes.

After all, you can't control the weather. But what you can control is whether you cancel or reschedule the party, hold the party regardless of rain, or host it at an indoor venue.

You can save a lot of time and energy—and build more mental strength—when you learn to focus on the things you can control. But before you make that shift, you have to learn to recognize when you're focusing on things that are completely out of your control.

Sometimes, things aren't completely cut and dry, however. In certain situations, you may have some control over the outcome, but not all. Take a minute to consider how much control you have over the following things. You may find there are plenty of things that you only have some control over, not complete control. Learning to recognize the factors within your control can help you put your energy into the right places. Place a checkmark in the box that depicts how much control you have over each situation:

	NO CONTROL	SOME CONTROL	COMPLETE CONTROL
How much sleep I get			
Getting a promotion			
My health			
My finances			
How much I exercise			

What Do You Waste Time Focusing On?

Take a few minutes to think about the types of things you waste time thinking about, worrying about, or talking about that you have no control over. Place a checkmark next to the things that sound familiar and see if you can fill in the blank with any things that aren't included on the list already.

☐ Things that already happened

☐ Future things I can't prevent

☐ Other people's behavior

☐ Mother nature (weather, natural disasters)

☐ World affairs (government rules, the economy, etc.)

☐ _____

> *No situation can have power over you without your reaction. Accept everything and enjoy today. And take care of your thoughts and the ocean of your mind. Master and control the waves inside you and you will be able to be happier in relation to absolutely everything that happens outside of you.*
>
> —Eduard Mateita (24, Romania)

Sierra's Story

Sierra started coming to therapy because she was in the middle of an ugly custody battle with her ex-husband. She had primary residence of their two boys and they visited with their father every weekend.

But Sierra was concerned about what went on at her ex-husband's house. She said, "He lets the kids stay up all hours of the night! They do whatever they want and then, when they come back home, they're out of control for a few days."

She spent a lot of time and energy reporting her ex-husband's behavior to the guardian ad litem, the attorney who had been appointed to look out for the best interest of the children. But she felt like the guardian ad litem wasn't as concerned as she should be.

For more than two years, Sierra had spent almost all of her time worrying about what happened at her ex-husband's home. It was consuming her and taking a toll on her relationship with the kids.

When she picked the kids up from their weekends with their dad, she peppered them with questions about what they did, how late they stayed up, what they ate, and what their father was doing. She could tell they were growing tired of her questions and clear disapproval of his rules, but she felt desperate to keep asking questions so she could find out what was going on when she wasn't there.

My treatment with her focused on letting go of the things she couldn't control—essentially all the things that happened at her ex-husband's house. Of course, if she had concerns that the children were being abused, she should step in and take action. But there wasn't much she could about the fact that her children had fewer rules at their father's home. Being allowed to stay up late and eat cookies for breakfast didn't constitute child abuse.

We worked on identifying what she could control (an exercise you'll learn about later in this chapter). She could control what happened in her home. She could also choose to invest her time into building a healthier relationship with her children.

I recommended she start scheduling time to worry—another exercise we'll cover shortly. She set aside fifteen minutes a day to worry about her children and what went on at their father's house. This was an effective strategy for her because she thought that as a devoted mom she should worry a little bit about what was happening over there but we didn't want those worries to consume her every waking minute.

At first, she found the changes difficult. She felt guilty for putting energy into things she enjoyed. She thought doing fun things while the kids weren't home (and not worrying about what they were doing) somehow meant she didn't care. But she also recognized that her children seemed more relaxed about coming back to her home when she stopped interrogating them about what happened at their dad's house.

Over the course of a few months, Sierra felt less stressed. Rather than focus on the things she thought her ex-husband was doing wrong, she invested her energy in doing the best she could. She started asking herself, "How did I do as a parent today?" and felt good about the things she was able to accomplish as a single mom.

Early on in treatment, whenever I asked how she was doing, she always replied by telling me something about her ex-husband and his latest "antics." But by the end of her treatment, she could reply to that question by telling me about how she was doing, because she was finally focusing on the things she could control.

Refusing to focus on things you can't control feels scary at first. But with consistent practice, you'll see how much you gain from only focusing on the things you can control. Here are my favorite exercises for building the mental strength you need to stop focusing on things you can't control.

Influence People but Don't Try to Control Them

You've probably heard people say things like, "You can't control other people." And there's truth in that. You can't make your partner clean the house, you can't make your mother stop drinking, and you can't make your child become a straight-A student.

> *I finally accepted that I can't make anyone act the way I want them to. It was scary in the beginning but it got better. My relationships got better too and I now have more time to worry about what I'm going to do.*
>
> —Matt G. (32, New Hampshire)

You can, however, influence people.

And when you stop focusing on trying to control them, you can begin paying attention to the influence you have on them.

Praising your child for cleaning their room increases the likelihood that they'll clean it again.

Changing the subject every time your friend begins to complain about the same thing over and over again reduces the chances that she'll keep bringing it up with you.

Role modeling healthy spending habits increases the chances your teenager will learn financial skills.

Not answering the phone after 10 P.M. reduces the chances that family will continuously call you late at night.

Who are some of the people whose behavior you have worried about to the extent that it wasn't helpful to you or them?

_____

_____

_____

_____

_____

Things that don't work

Take a minute and think about the ways in which you've tried to change other people's behavior in the past that weren't effective. Place a checkmark next to these strategies that likely didn't work so well and fill in the blank if you have any other things you tried that weren't a good idea.

☐ Lecturing people

☐ Giving out unsolicited advice

☐ Complaining about someone's behavior to other people

☐ Nagging or pleading

☐ Giving ultimatums you don't follow through on

☐ Establishing boundaries that are meant to change other people rather than preserve your inner peace

☐ _____

Things that do work

Think about things you've tried that have had a healthy influence on people around you. Maybe you supported someone who wanted to change their habits or perhaps you praised someone for trying something new. Place a checkmark next to the healthy ways you've tried to influence people and fill in the blank if you can think of any strategies that aren't on the list already:

☐ Establishing boundaries that are for you (protecting your time, energy, inner peace) as opposed to trying to manipulate the other person

☐ Role modeling healthy behaviors

☐ Giving people space to find their own solutions

☐ Supporting people in their efforts to change

☐ Providing resources that could help someone

☐ Praising positive behavior

☐ Ignoring negative behavior

☐ Asking questions to help people determine what they want

☐ Listening to someone who is trying to find their own solution

☐ _____

You can establish a goal for yourself based on your behavior. So you might start showing more gratitude when your partner acts lovingly toward you. Or you might commit to avoid lecturing your sibling about their choices and instead, point out the positive things they're doing.

At the end of the day, you can ask yourself how you did. Regardless of whether the other person's behavior changed, you can control your behavior.

Think of someone who you would like to influence. What healthy steps could you take to try and be a positive influence in their life?

_____

_____

_____

_____

_____

Replace Problem Thoughts with Solution Thoughts

Another reason you might get stuck focusing on things you can't control is that you spend all your time dwelling on the problem, rather than looking for a solution.

Developing solutions is helpful. Dwelling on the problem isn't. Here are some examples of the differences:

Problem thought: I'm going to mess up in this interview.

Solution thought: I can practice developing answers to sample interview questions.

Problem thought: I'll be so embarrassed if my mother drinks too much at her retirement party.

Solution thought: If she starts drinking, I'll leave the party.

It's easy to get caught up in rehashing the problem over and over again. But thinking about the problem longer and harder won't lead to a better solution When you find yourself dwelling on a problem, work on responding with a solution thought.

What's an example of a problem thought you have and a solution thought you can respond to it with?

Problem thought: _____

_____

_____

_____

_____

Solution thought: _____

_____

_____

_____

_____

When do you tend to focus on problem thoughts?

_____

_____

_____

_____

_____

How can you remind yourself to respond to them with solution thoughts?

_____

_____

_____

_____

_____

Identify One Thing You Can Control

In my second book, *13 Things Mentally Strong Parents Don't Do,* I talked about how parents can let kids feel as though they have a sense of control over some things in their lives. For example, you might ask your child, "Do you want water or ice water to drink?" That small choice about whether to add ice to their water gives them a sense of autonomy.

But there are situations in which kids have very little control over what happens to them. And I cite an extreme example—kids undergoing intrusive cancer treatments. Young kids don't understand why they're being poked, prodded, put in machines, and being subjected to painful procedures. Often, nurses and doctors have to hold them down to administer these life-saving procedures that feel really painful.

Kids reported high pain levels while undergoing various procedures. So experts taught them breathing exercises. Then, no matter what they were subjected to, they had control over something—how they breathed. And suddenly, they started ranking their pain lower. It's proof that you can always find something within your control and when you do, you'll start to feel better.

Whether you are subjected to less than an ideal work environment or you have a loved one with a serious health problem, there are always some things you can control—your effort, your attitude, and your own behavior.

Fill in the circles below to reflect what you have control over and what you don't. On the inner circle, include things you can control (like your behavior). In the outer circle, write down things you can't control (like the economy). This visual can remind you what to stay focused on.

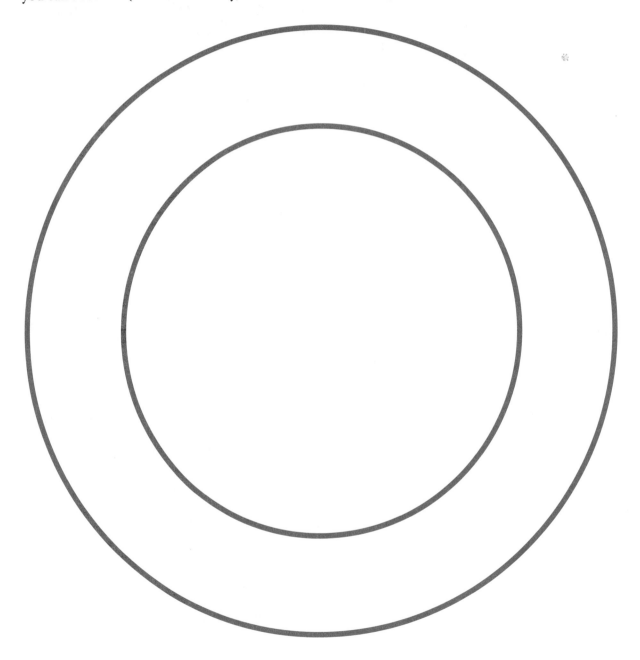

What's something you've recently worried about that you have no control over?

_____

_____

_____

_____

_____

_____

What's one thing you can control in that situation?

_____

_____

_____

_____

_____

_____

> _When I find myself worrying about something a lot, I just ask myself how much this thing is going to matter in five years. The truth is, it probably won't matter at all so it's pointless to waste today worrying about something like that._
>
> —Don S. (56, Alabama)

Schedule Time to Worry

It sounds ridiculous on the surface. If you worry a lot, why would you schedule more time to worry?

Well, there's research that shows setting aside a few minutes every day to worry can help you contain your worrying to your specified time.

Here's how it works:

Schedule twenty minutes to worry every day at a specific time.

When you find yourself worrying outside of your scheduled worry time, remind yourself, "It's not time to worry about that yet. I'll worry about that later."

When your worrying time rolls around, sit down and worry as much as you can.

You might sit on the couch and think about all the things bothering you. Or you might write in a journal about all the worries that come to mind.

When your time is up, go do something else.

With practice, you can train your brain to worry for twenty minutes rather than all day every day.

My therapy clients who try this report it takes them a couple of weeks to feel better, but with daily practice, they worry far less. Some of them even look physically transformed as if the weight of the world has literally been lifted off their shoulders.

If you spend a lot of time focusing on things you can't control, schedule time to worry. Most people find it works better to do this later in the day so they can put their worrying off until evening. Just make sure you don't do it right before you go to sleep though. Worrying too much at bedtime might make it harder to sleep.

How could scheduling time to worry benefit you?

_____

_____

_____

_____

_____

Set aside twenty minutes every day to worry as an experiment. Try it for two weeks and see what you notice.

This Week's Homework

When you find yourself trying to fix something or when you are worrying a lot about something, pause and ask yourself, "Is this within my control?" If not, find something that is within your control and see how much better you feel when you keep putting your energy to good use.

Create Your Plan to Stop Focusing on Things You Can't Control

What are some things you can do to stop focusing on things you can't control?

☐ Focus on my behavior

☐ Replace problem thoughts with solution thoughts

☐ Write down things I can control and read over that list

☐ Schedule time to worry about things I can't control

☐ Put more effort into influencing people, rather than controlling them

☐ _____

Now identify some clear action steps you can take to stop focusing on things you can't control. Here are some examples:

➤ When I'm worried about something, I'll start asking myself, "What part of this problem is within my control?"

➤ Every day I'll remind myself of at least one thing that is within my control.

➤ I'll limit the amount of time I spend watching the news so I won't get as anxious about things I can't control.

➤ If my family member tries to talk about politics, I'll change the subject.

➤ When I start to worry about someone else's choices, I'll take a breath and remind myself my job is to be a good role model. Their behavior is their choice.

What's one step you can take to start focusing only on the things you can control?

_____

_____

_____

_____

_____

_____

What will you notice about yourself once you start focusing on the things you can control?

_____

_____

_____

_____

_____

_____

How will your life be different?

_____

_____

_____

_____

_____

When I **STOPPED** pleasing everyone . . .

I gave myself permission to say no and be OK with myself after.

—Amy Woodley (36, Canada)

The weight I had been carrying on my shoulders was lifted away and I was able to focus on my health and what I needed to do to become a better version of me.

—Jason Smith (35, Colorado)

I started paying attention to what I wanted out of life. I realized it was my job to make myself happy and I didn't need other people to like my choices.

—Victoria Alan (31, New York)

Don't Worry About Pleasing Everyone

MANY READERS HAVE described themselves to me as "lifelong people pleasers." Whether they were always saying yes to everything asked of them or they were abandoning what they wanted in an effort to appease those around them, they felt responsible for how other people felt.

Breaking free from people pleasing isn't easy. But it gives you the inner peace and freedom you may have been trying to gain from trying to make everyone else happy. The truth is you aren't responsible for anyone else's happiness. And when you learn to focus on living according to your values, you'll get comfortable enough in your own skin to resist the urge to people please.

How Do You Try to Please Everyone?

In this chapter we'll discuss the reasons why you might be a people pleaser, how it could play out in your life, and the exercises that can help you stop trying to do it. Before we look at what to do about the issue, let's examine the ways in which you might be trying to please everyone. Take a look at the following statements and place a checkmark next to the ones that sound like you.

☐ I say yes to things I don't want to do.

☐ I pretend to agree with people even when I don't.

☐ I answer questions by saying, "I don't care," even when I do.

☐ I do things that I think will make other people like me more.

☐ I worry about posting on social media because I don't want to offend anyone.

☐ I have trouble making decisions because I worry about what other people might think.

☐ I only share my opinions when I know the other person will agree.

☐ I try hard to fit in with the people around me.

☐ I automatically say yes to everything that is asked of me.

☐ I spend a lot of time trying to guess how other people are feeling and make my decisions based on what I think will make them happiest.

What are some examples of ways you've gotten caught up in people pleasing?

_____
_____
_____
_____
_____

What types of thoughts contributed to people pleasing?

_____
_____
_____
_____
_____

How do you feel when you're trying to please everyone?

_____
_____
_____
_____
_____

People Pleasing vs. Being Kind

Readers of *13 Things Mentally Strong People Don't Do* will occasionally ask me things like, "But, shouldn't I want to please some people in my life?" Of course. Maybe you surprise your partner with a gift you know they'll like. Or maybe you choose to help your friend with a household project even though there are a million other ways you'd rather spend a Saturday.

Doing kind things for others out of the goodness of your heart is one thing. Losing sight of who you are in an effort to try and make everyone around you happy is different.

PEOPLE PLEASING	BEING KIND
Acting out of guilt or fear	Acting out of genuine desire to be helpful
Feeling responsible for other people's feelings	Allowing others to take responsibility for feelings
Feeling like you're being taken advantage of	Setting limits
Saying yes to things out of a sense of obligation	Saying yes to things that are in line with your values
Setting own needs aside	Honoring own needs and balancing it with the needs of others

What's an example of a time when you thought you were being kind but you were actually people pleasing?

_____

_____

_____

_____

_____

But trying to make other people happy—at the expense of your own well-being—is a losing battle. You can't "make" anyone feel happy. The best way to have a positive influence on people is to be the best version of yourself, not a copycat version of them.

> _When someone else's life isn't going well or they aren't happy, I want to spring into action and fix things. But doing that too many times has taught me nothing good comes out of it. I can support people but it's not my job to try and make them happy. They have to do that for themselves._
>
> —Brianna Foster (31, Nevada)

Why Do You Try to Please Everyone?

From deep-rooted insecurities to habits you've slowly developed over time, there are many reasons why you might become a people pleaser. Take a few minutes and think about the reasons you've tried to please people. Place a checkmark next to the things that sound familiar and fill in the blank line with any other reasons that weren't already mentioned.

- ☐ It makes me feel good (temporarily).
- ☐ I want people to like me.
- ☐ I am afraid people will reject me if I don't do what they want.
- ☐ I am afraid of conflict.
- ☐ I'm terrified people will leave me.
- ☐ It takes too much energy to speak up.
- ☐ I don't want to appear selfish.
- ☐ It's just easier to do what other people want.
- ☐ I don't even know what I want.
- ☐ _____

What uncomfortable emotion are you trying to avoid when you try to please people?

_____

_____

_____

_____

_____

Brandon came into my office at the urging of his wife, Anita. She attended the appointment with him so she could tell me her concerns.

One of the reasons Anita fell in love with Brandon was because he was so generous and kind. But over the years, she grew frustrated by the fact that he was always helping everyone else. Sometimes, she felt like it was at her expense.

They had plenty of projects that he could be doing around the house. But Anita said she felt like she had to take a number and get in line before she could get a leaky faucet fixed or a light fixture replaced.

It caused tension in their relationship. Anita thought Brandon needed to say no more often to other people. Brandon didn't agree with Anita's concerns but he loved his wife and agreed to go to therapy.

One of the exercises we did in treatment involved clarifying Brandon's values (an exercise you'll learn about a little later in this chapter). Brandon's marriage was important to him. Helping people was also important to him, but he didn't want to do it at the expense of his relationship.

But one problem was that he felt like people depended on his help. Whether it was an elderly neighbor who wanted his help installing a new dishwasher or it was a family member who wanted assistance building a new patio, he felt compelled to say yes.

So we started talking about how every "yes" meant he was saying "no" to something else. Whenever he agreed to help someone, he was saying no to spending time with his wife or doing something she asked of him.

When he framed it this way in his head, his behavior changed. He was able to start saying "yes" more often to his own needs and his wife's needs. That meant he had to decline other opportunities sometimes, but it also meant he could live according to his values with a high priority on his relationship.

It only took a few sessions for Brandon to create changes in his behavior. He reported less tension at home and a happier relationship with his wife once he stopped trying to please everyone.

I learned to own my decisions and stick up for them. There's not always one right action in a situation. I make the best decision I can with the information I have. I may do different next time, but next time I will have the information from this experience.

—Ashley (29, Oregon)

Mental Strength Exercises

If you fall into the people-pleasing trap often, there are plenty of exercises that can help you build mental strength. As you grow mentally stronger, you'll develop the courage you need to live according to your own values and you'll be able to tolerate the uncomfortable feelings that can arise when others aren't happy with your choices. Here are some of my favorite exercises that can put a stop to trying to please everyone.

Separate Self-Care from Being Selfish

There's a big difference between taking care of yourself and being selfish. But sometimes, people take the idea that they're not out to please everyone a little too far in the other direction. It's important to honor your own needs while also considering the needs of those around you.

Here are some scenarios to consider how you might strike that balance.

Following through with commitments

We all overcommit ourselves sometimes. And there are times when backing out of a commitment makes sense. You might decline an invitation after you've accepted or you might have to tell someone you can't get all the work done by the deadline. And sometimes, those actions will have little effect on anyone else. In reality, no one might be bothered that you didn't show up for that networking event you said you would attend. In those cases, changing your mind might be an example of healthy self-care.

But if you made a promise, following through with your promise isn't necessarily people pleasing; it's being true to your word. But I see a lot of people backing out of commitments and calling it self-care, even though their last-second change of heart affects other people. So there may be times when you decide to push yourself to go even though you don't feel like it because it's the right thing to do. Ultimately, you could chalk it up to a learning experience that prevents you from overcommitting yourself in the future.

How often do you overcommit yourself? What steps can you take to work on this?

_____

_____

_____

_____

_____

Being Honest

Consider your values surrounding kindness and honesty. For example, let's say someone asks, "How do you like my new shirt?" You don't like it. Do you say it looks great to please them? Do you get brutally honest and say you hate it? Or do you give an answer that is somewhere in the middle, like, "It fits great. It's kind of bright, though."?

You don't need to say what people want to hear. But on the other hand, you don't always need to share your entire opinion if it's going to hurt someone's feelings. Think about how you might find the balance between being honest and being kind in the following situations:

Your colleague asks, "Did you like that presentation I gave in the meeting today?" You thought it was boring. What could you say?

_____

_____

_____

_____

_____

Your friend says they are thinking of quitting their job to become an artist. You think it sounds like a huge risk. They really want to know what you think. What would you say?

_____

_____

_____

_____

_____

It's not your job to tell people what they want to hear. However, you also don't need to be brutally honest when your opinion won't be helpful to someone. Figuring out where to draw the line can be more of an art than a science, however.

Clarify Your Values

People pleasing often stems from not knowing your values. After all, it's hard to stick to a plan if you're constantly sidetracked by someone else's opinions of what's important. But when you know what your values are, it's easier to tune out other people's input.

A few years ago, I hosted a workshop at a school. During the day, I met with the middle school students. I asked them, "Would your parents rather that your teacher said you are the smartest kid in the class or the kindest kid?" Almost every kid in the audience said their parent would prefer they be the smartest kid.

That evening, I met with the parents. I asked them which they would rather hear—that their kid was the smartest or the kindest. Almost every parent said they would prefer kindest. I challenged them to go home and ask their kids what they thought they preferred.

There's no right or wrong answer to the question about whether you'd prefer to raise the kindest kid in the class or the smartest. But it's important to know what your answer is so you can ensure you're living according to your values.

It's likely that many of those parents asked their kids about homework and grades a lot more than they asked them about how kind they were at recess. So even if they valued kindness the most, they may not be acting like it.

Focus on what really matters. If your child is doing their homework and a peer calls crying, is it OK to stop working to help someone? Or should they call their friend back later once their work is done?

There are lots of worksheets out there that ask you to pick what you value most, but many of them overcomplicate things. After all, how do you decide which is more important: honesty or respect? They go hand in hand.

So here's a simple values clarification exercise. Think about these four major domains in your life and consider how you value them:

1. *Work/volunteering:* How important is your paid employment, caring for family, volunteer work, and things you do for your community? How important are these things to you? What qualities do you bring to your work? How fulfilling is your work?

   _____
   _____
   _____
   _____
   _____

2. *Relationships:* How much do you value relationships with immediate family, extended family, friends, coworkers, and other social contacts? What type of relationship changes would you want to make? What personal qualities do you bring to those relationships?

   _____
   _____
   _____
   _____
   _____

3. *Wellness:* How much time do you want to devote to your spiritual wellness, mental health, physical health, and anything related to self-improvement and wellbeing?

   _____
   _____
   _____
   _____
   _____

4. *Leisure:* How important is it that you have time to play and relax? Do you have hobbies, leisure activities, and creative outlets?

_____

_____

_____

_____

_____

What else do you place a high value on? Money? Making a contribution to society? Describe some other things that are important to you.

_____

_____

_____

_____

_____

Does your time and the way you spend your money reflect that you value those things?

_____

_____

_____

_____

_____

When are you tempted to compromise your values to make someone else happy?

_____

_____

_____

_____

How can keeping your values in mind prevent you from being a people pleaser?

_____

_____

_____

_____

Identify People You Can Talk To

When you're thinking about a decision, like whether to move or whether to buy a car, you don't need to survey everyone around you to ensure they're on the same page.

But bouncing an idea off a trusted friend or family member can be helpful. This is especially true with emotional decisions. Your emotions can cloud your judgment.

Asking someone else to weigh in can help you see potential risks you might be overlooking or potential benefits you might be discounting.

It's important to note that not everyone is qualified to give you advice in all areas of your life. Your grandmother might offer a lot of wisdom in the relationship department, but that doesn't mean you should follow her business advice. In general, though, try to identify who really has your best interest at heart. These are the core people you can turn to when you're struggling. That doesn't mean it's your job to try and please them, but it does mean you might take their opinion into consideration.

Who are the five people whose opinions you truly value and what type of advice would you most likely to turn to them for (business, financial, friendship, romantic, home-improvement, general life advice, etc.)?

1. _____

2. _____

3. _____

4. _____

5. _____

> *I felt a complete sense of relief. I needed to recognize it wasn't healthy to please people all the time and not assess how my "yes" would affect me. Now I try to reflect on my motivation before saying yes or doing something that might be people pleasing. I desire to serve people and have a lot of empathy, but it is important to have balance.*
>
> —Casey Morlet (36, California)

Develop a Mantra

Create a quick little catchphrase to repeat to yourself when you're tempted to please people. It can drown out the negative thoughts and help reduce some of those uncomfortable feelings—like anxiety or sadness.

It can also prevent you from engaging in your go-to people-pleasing habits. If you tend to say yes to everything asked of you, your mantra might be "pause and think." Repeating that phrase to yourself as someone is asking you a favor might prevent you from agreeing to do things you don't want to do. Instead of giving an automatic yes, you might be able to say, "I'll think about that and get back to you."

I once worked with a woman whose mantra became "self-respect." She had a partner who made unreasonable demands on her. And she often gave in because she wanted to avoid conflict. But once she started repeating "self-respect" to herself often enough, she was able to say no when he bossed her around. She said it reminded her that her job was to treat herself with respect, even if he didn't, and it helped her stop trying to make him happy.

Here are some examples of other mantras that could help you stop trying to please everyone:

- My feelings count.

- My opinion matters.

- I'm allowed to say no.

- I can handle people being angry.

- No one else has to like it.

- Just breathe.

- They don't have to like me. It's more important that I like me.

Now it's your turn to develop a personal mantra. You can certainly borrow from the above list. Or you can create your own little catchphrase that you can repeat to yourself whenever you're tempted to please people.

What is your mantra going to be? When is your mantra likely to be most helpful to you?

_____

_____

_____

_____

_____

When you say yes to things this week, ask yourself what you're also saying no to. It might mean anything from TV time with the family to going to the gym. But if yes has become your default answer to almost everything, it can be helpful to get into the habit of identifying what you're also saying no to in life.

Create Your Plan to Stop Pleasing Everyone

What are some things you can do to stop trying to please everyone?

☐ Get clearer on my values

☐ Say no to requests I don't want to do

☐ Share my opinion

☐ Speak up when my feelings are hurt

☐ Ask for things I need

☐ Set healthy boundaries with people

☐ Practice tolerating the discomfort felt when people are upset with me

☐ _____

Now identify some clear action steps you can begin to take. These small steps can go a long way toward helping you live according to your values, even when other people aren't happy with your choices. Here are some examples of small steps you might take:

➤ When my friend tries to pressure me into going out after I've said no, I'll say no again firmly.

➤ When my daughter tries to guilt me into loaning her money, I'll say no.

➤ When my colleague asks me to do a favor because they didn't do their own work, I'll decline.

➤ When my friends ask me where I want to eat lunch, I'll suggest a restaurant rather than say, "I don't care."

➤ I'll stop asking for other people's opinions on what I should do about my job situation, and I'll make up my own mind based on what I think is best.

What's one step you can take to stop trying to please everyone?

_____

_____

_____

_____

_____

_____

What will you notice about yourself once you stop trying to please everyone?

_____

_____

_____

_____

_____

_____

How will your life be different if you stop trying to please everyone?

_____

_____

_____

_____

_____

_____

When I **STOPPED** being afraid of taking calculated risks . . .

I started to view every challenge or obstacle as an opportunity to grow and discover and learn more about myself and what I am capable/incapable of. This has helped me know what I should focus on and what needs more attention/work. I learned to view every opportunity as a lesson and there's always something learned in the end.

—Sara Al Yasin (22, West Virginia)

I realized things turn out way better than I predict.

—Bruce Monteiro (53, California)

I felt like I was really living for the first time ever. It was scary, fun, and exciting. I actually feel more in control now because I don't waste time worrying about bad things that might happen anymore.

—Anthony Rivas (43, New York)

Don't
Fear Taking
Calculated Risks

IT'S NORMAL TO enjoy risks in certain areas of your life, but not others. One person might like financial risks but struggle to take social risks. Another might look forward to physical risks (triathlons and mountain climbing) but can't imagine taking a career risk.

One of my therapy clients once asked me, "Why do people say you should step outside your comfort zone? I am uncomfortable all the time already. All I want is to feel better." With treatment, he was able to recognize how his desire to get comfortable and avoid risks was actually the root of his problem. Taking a few more chances in life gave him confidence that he could handle being uncomfortable sometimes.

A happy life doesn't stem from the absence of risk or challenges. In fact, a lot of wisdom and strength develops from the challenges we accept.

How Do You Avoid Taking Calculated Risks?

In this chapter, I'll explain why you might embrace some risks and not others. I'll also teach you how to calculate risks so you can reduce your fear and increase your courage. Before we start looking at what to do about risk, let's figure out how risk aversion plays out in your life. Take a few minutes to review the following statements and place a checkmark next to the ones that sound familiar.

☐ I avoid anything that feels scary.

☐ I keep my money in the places that feel safest (the bank, low-risk retirement accounts, etc.).

☐ I am slow to let people get to know me because I think it's risky to tell others about my personal life.

☐ I have trouble turning acquaintances into friends because I am never sure if people really like me.

☐ Once I get going on something, I don't like to quit even when it's not going well because I don't want to waste all the time and effort I've put in.

☐ I am not likely to ask for a raise, apply for a promotion, or try to advance my career too much because I'm afraid I'll get turned down.

☐ When people tell me about the businesses they're starting or the big goals they're setting, I immediately think about all the things that could go wrong.

What's an example of a risk that felt really scary (regardless of whether you took it)?

_____

_____

_____

_____

_____

What did you think about that risk and your chances of success?

_____

_____

_____

_____

_____

How did those thoughts and feelings influence your behavior?

_____

_____

_____

_____

_____

Avoiding Risks vs. Taking Too Many Risks

While some people go to great lengths to avoid anything that seems even slightly risky, other people impulsively leap at every chance they get.

The reason for these two extremes is often the same—the desire to avoid discomfort. For some people, investigating stock options feels overwhelming. Rather than spend countless anxiety-filled hours trying to learn about their options, they throw all their money at something and hope it works out.

> *I always remind myself that it could go better than I possibly imagine. And oftentimes when considering the real downside or consequence of taking a risk, I find it isn't as bad as I have built it up to be.*
>
> —Maddie Smith (22, Iowa)

Similarly, other people might jump at the chance to try an alternative treatment for a health issue without looking at the potential risks. They might think investigating the downside would raise their concern—so they might as well bury their head in the sand and not look.

It's important to be an informed risk-tasker. When you learn how to calculate risk and you're confident in your ability to handle the outcome, you can challenge yourself to create your best life.

Why Do You Fear Taking Calculated Risks?

Whether we're talking about a social risk or a financial risk, taking the leap can be tough. But everybody's reasons for dodging risks are different. Take a few minutes to think about why you fear taking calculated risks and check off the ones that apply to you.

- ☐ I think rejection, embarrassment, and failure are intolerable.
- ☐ I would rather keep my anxiety low than take a risk that might not pay off.
- ☐ I spend a lot of time thinking about potential worst-case scenarios.
- ☐ I believe I have bad luck.
- ☐ I have been hurt before and I don't want to risk getting hurt again.

☐ I overestimate the chances of something going wrong.

☐ I underestimate my ability to handle a failed outcome.

☐ _____

> *Baby steps! At first it was just speaking up in a meeting. I was always so scared to do this, as I thought I would say something that would make me look unqualified. Once you do this a few times and realize it is OK to speak up, you are more confident to do it in the future. You learn that everyone has something to contribute and it's OK to be vulnerable.*
>
> —Heather Tabin (57, Canada)

Christy's Story

Christy came into my therapy office because she felt depressed. She was thirty-five, lived alone, had a steady job, and for the most part, she liked her life. She felt frustrated by lingering depression. Although it wasn't severe, she never really found relief from it.

We spent several weeks talking about her symptoms and the problems it caused for her. As I got to know her, one thing was clear: she was actually a fairly anxious person. But she did a great job of avoiding things that caused her to feel anxious.

Social situations caused anxiety for her. So she'd created a life that allowed her to avoid a lot of social contact. She worked from home. She conducted most of her business online. When she did need to leave home to go to the grocery store, for example, she shopped at a store that was open twenty-four hours a day so she could go in the middle of the night when few people were there.

She had a couple of close friends and she usually invited them to her place to watch a movie or eat dinner. Every once in a while they'd convince her to go to the movies or go to a restaurant.

Essentially, she'd created a lifestyle that helped her manage her anxiety well. Unfortunately, that same lifestyle increased her risk of depression. Her days were very predictable. And she rarely took any type of risks.

She spent her entire existence playing defense. To ensure nothing bad would happen, she played everything safe. She frequently said things like, "I don't want to buy a house because the housing market might plummet," and "I don't want to waste time dating because relationships rarely work out anyway."

Once these patterns became clear (Christy hadn't even realized she was doing it), we explored why it was so important to her to play it safe. It turns out, she was raised by a mom who had a lot of anxiety. Her mother pointed out the worst-case scenarios in everything. She warned Christy about horrible things that could happen, even things that were unlikely—like contracting rare diseases or getting kidnapped by a stranger. She sheltered Christy from being able to do a lot of normal activities, like playing in the park or going to friends' homes.

From a young age Christy learned the best way to prevent bad things from happening was to always play it safe. Playing it safe also helped her avoid uncertainty and normal feelings of anxiety that might accompany healthy risks, like investing money or going on a date.

In treatment, she worked on learning to tolerate anxiety, a little at a time. We talked about the symptoms she experienced when she had anxiety and the skills she could use to deal with those physical and emotional symptoms.

We also discussed "false alarms"—an exercise I'll share later in this chapter. Essentially, this helped her recognize how both her body and her brain sometimes responded to minor inconveniences as if they were a life-and-death situation. Understanding that she wasn't in any actual danger helped her tolerate those symptoms better.

She started taking little risks one small step at a time. She went out of the house a little more often. She challenged herself to meet new people. And she began trying some new things.

It wasn't easy for her to do. It caused her to experience a fair amount of anxiety. But being more active helped her depression and she pushed herself to keep working at it.

Over the course of several months, Christy made a lot of progress. She joined a yoga class, started volunteering at a local animal shelter, and made plans to go on a weekend trip with a friend. By the end of our work together, she had confidence that she could take some risks in life. And she also felt confident that she could handle risks even when they didn't turn out the way she wanted. She knew that feeling a little anxious and uncertain wasn't as bad as she had thought.

Mental Strength Exercises

It's important to build confidence in yourself if you want to stop fearing calculated risks. Fortunately, there are lots of exercises that can help you get better at calculating risks and help you manage the anxiety that comes with risk-taking. Here are my favorite exercises for building the mental strength you need to get comfortable with taking calculated risks.

Recognize Your Anxiety Alarm

We all have anxiety alarms. They're supposed to ring when we're in danger. When the alarm goes off, your brain tells your body to be on high alert. Then you can take whatever action you need to stay safe.

That'd be helpful if you were in a life-and-death situation. Your anxiety alarm bell would save your life.

In today's world, though, we don't face the same life-and-death situations our ancestors did. You aren't sleeping in a cave with hungry predators lurking around the corner. But your brain might still respond to stressful situations as if they were deadly threats. Most of us have fairly faulty anxiety alarms these days. They ring when our friend doesn't text back right away or they go off the second we get an email from the boss that reads, "Let's meet" even though your life doesn't depend on your friend replying or on keeping your job.

It's easy to think that if we feel really anxious something must be really risky—even though that's not true. That's why it's important to test your anxiety alarm.

What happens to your body when your anxiety alarm bell rings?

☐ Heart races

☐ Can't think clearly

☐ Face feels flushed

☐ Stomach feels sick

☐ Breathing is short and rapid

☐ Feel dizzy

☐ _____

What's an example of a time when you experienced a false alarm?

_____

_____

_____

_____

_____

Old Anxiety Alarms That Keep Ringing

We all experience false anxiety alarms. Sometimes it's easy to recognize a false alarm—and the reason for it—right away. At other times, it's a little more difficult.

My own anxiety alarm bell took me a bit to piece together, partly because it was so strange. The second I hear *The Simpsons* theme song, my alarm bell goes off. Just typing that caused me to play the beginning of the song in my head and as soon as I did, my stomach did a somersault. But no matter where I am, if there's a TV in another room and I hear that theme song play, I immediately begin to feel physically ill, despite the fact as a kid, I really liked that show.

Here's why—I hated school as a kid. Whenever a concerned teacher or my parents tried to get me to identify what exactly I hated about it, I couldn't. All I could say was, "It's a really long day." And that was true. One school day felt like four years.

At some points, I hated school so much I threw up in the morning.

I loved Friday nights because it meant I didn't have to go to school for two whole days! That was the best feeling ever.

But I knew the weekend was coming to a close on Sunday night when *The Simpsons* came on TV. Hearing that theme song meant it was almost Monday morning—and I was about to have five really long school days ahead of me.

As luck would have it, *The Simpsons* has become the longest running show in television and it still plays on Sunday nights. And even though I haven't had to go to school on a Monday morning in a really long time, my anxiety alarm still rings loudly the second that theme song comes on.

These days I can quickly remind myself it's a false alarm. My body simply reacts to the theme song the same way Pavlov's dogs drooled when they heard a bell ring. And while it's annoying that it still happens, it's not a big deal. I just remind myself that my brain and my body associate the song with school, and I turn it into an opportunity to practice gratitude about the fact that I don't ever have to go to school again.

Some people experience alarms after much more traumatic experiences. If something bad happened to you when there was a certain song playing in the background, that song might trigger your body's alarm every time you hear it. Or if something bad happened to you when there was a pumpkin spice–scented candle burning nearby, that smell might also trigger an alarm even when you're completely safe. If you experience false alarms that stem from trauma, consider getting professional help if you can. A mental health professional maybe be able to help retrain your brain and your body to address the alarm bells that can interfere with living your best life.

Do you have any sights, sounds, tastes, or experiences that trigger your body's alarm bells even when you're safe?

_____

_____

_____

_____

_____

Your False Alarms

False alarms aren't just associated with bad memories and traumatic experiences, however.

You might find if you're asked to give a presentation in front of a hundred people, your brain and your body reacts the same way it would if you were dangling off the edge of a cliff—even though public speaking doesn't actually put you in any physical danger.

Or maybe you replay a conversation in your head over and over again and second-guess everything you said earlier in the day. You might find yourself suddenly questioning whether you offended the other person or whether you said something that caused you to look foolish. All this thinking might cause you to start feeling a tightening in your chest—a surefire sign that your anxiety alarm bell is ringing.

Anxiety alarm bells feel uncomfortable. So they often affect our behavior. We might rush through a presentation or skip it altogether. Or we might repeatedly ask someone for reassurance that something we did was acceptable. Ultimately, those alarm bells can scare us into avoiding risks—even the healthy ones.

What kinds of circumstances cause you to experience false anxiety alarms?

_____

_____

_____

_____

What action do you take (or avoid)?

_____

_____

_____

_____

_____

Raise Your Logic

Sometimes we're afraid of all the wrong things. We assume that our level of fear is equal to the level of risk. In reality, our level of anxiety has nothing to do with the actual level of risk you face.

What feels scarier, driving a car five miles down the road or giving a speech in front of a thousand people?

If you're like most people, you'd say the speech feels scarier. In reality, you face a much higher risk of death or injury driving your car than you do standing onstage. But most of us wouldn't think twice about getting in a car—and most of us would do just about anything to avoid public speaking.

> The best advice I ever received was "do it scared." I don't have to wait for all my fear to go away before taking action. Instead, I can feel scared and do it anyway.
>
> Elana J. (48, Texas)

Recognizing that your fear is irrational and unwarranted can help you keep things in perspective. Not only might it reduce your anxiety but it can also give you confidence that you can tolerate the anxiety.

Intellectually knowing that something isn't dangerous might not always decrease your anxiety. But it can increase your courage. I'm much more willing to face a fear when I know the actual risk level.

I live on a sailboat. Every once in a while, someone has to climb to the top of the sailboat mast 64 feet in the air to either replace a light bulb or fix the wind indicator (which shows which way the wind is blowing). I usually volunteer to do it because I feel less anxious doing it myself rather than watching Steve go up there (after being widowed once, I'd rather not watch Steve do anything that looks scary). I don't like heights but there are several safety ropes that make it a fairly safe venture. Reminding myself that climbing up there with safety lines attached is likely safer than driving to the grocery store helps me find the courage I need to do it, even though it still feels scary. So while my fear level is about a 9/10, knowing my actual level risk is more like a 2/10 gives me the courage to do it.

It's helpful to see how your fear level is out of proportion to the actual level of physical danger you are in. Spend a few minutes thinking about how scary these activities feel versus how much physical danger they actually put you in.

EVENT	FEAR LEVEL 1–10	ESTIMATED PHYSICAL RISK 1–10
Driving five miles	1	3
Giving a speech to a thousand people		
First day at a new job		
Inviting acquaintance for coffee		
Attending a networking event alone		

Fill in the chart below to include some events in your life that feel riskier than they actually are.

EVENT	FEAR LEVEL 1–10	ESTIMATED PHYSICAL RISK 1–10

How can you remind yourself to examine the actual level of risk you face rather than simply allow your level of fear to dictate your choices?

_____

_____

_____

_____

_____

Create an If . . . Then Plan

You might find you avoid risks that are likely to set off your anxiety alarm. Going to a networking event, attending an appointment with a therapist, or enrolling in a class might be things you decline to do because you don't want to feel anxious.

But the truth is, feeling anxious (or another uncomfortable emotion) isn't the end of the world. And research shows you'll tolerate it much better if you develop an if . . . then plan for yourself.

For example, you might avoid giving a presentation because you're afraid you'll feel so nervous that you'll forget what you want to say.

So a good if . . . then plan would be: If I get nervous, then I'll pause, take a deep breath, and look at my notes.

Here are some more examples—try to fill in the rest of the chart:

IF . . .	THEN . . .
If I don't know what to say when I'm talking to someone,	then I'll ask a question about where they grew up.
If no one talks to me at this networking event,	then I will walk up to someone and introduce myself.
If my coworker interrupts me,	then I'll say, "I wasn't finished," and continue talking.
If I feel nervous when I make that phone call,	

IF . . .	THEN . . .
If the interviewer asks me a question I don't know how to answer,	
If someone starts talking about an uncomfortable subject at the family event,	
If I feel like my doctor isn't listening to me when I share my concerns,	

Think of some things in your life that you've declined to do because you were afraid your anxiety alarm bell would go off. Now create an if . . . then plan that could help you get through it.

_____

_____

_____

_____

_____

Identify a small risk you want to take this week. It could be anything from joining the gym you've been afraid to join or inviting an old friend for coffee—whatever sounds a little risky to you. Pay attention to the thoughts that pop into your head when you think about that risk. Notice your emotions. And practice facing your fear and taking that risk. Then, pay attention to what you learned about yourself in the process.

Create Your Plan to Stop Fearing Calculated Risks

What are steps you can take to stop fearing calculated risks?

☐ Begin recognizing my false anxiety alarms

☐ Start viewing risk with more logic and less emotion

☐ Create an if . . . then plan to help me handle whatever outcome I face

☐ Practice taking one small risk at a time

☐ Take steps to reduce the risks I face

☐ Educate myself so I am less fearful of a risk

☐ _____

Now identify one small action step you can take to tackle your fear of risk head-on. Here are some examples of steps someone might take to reduce the fear of risks.

➤ I will start researching retirement plan options so I can feel more comfortable investing my money.

➤ I will invite one person for a social activity once per week.

➤ I will invite a friend to go with me to the gym the first time I go so that I can get started working out.

➤ I will practice making one phone a call day until talking on the phone doesn't feel so scary anymore.

What's one step you can take that will help you take more calculated risks?

_____

_____

_____

_____

_____

_____

What will you notice about yourself once you start taking more calculated risks?

_____

_____

_____

_____

_____

_____

What will be different about your life?

_____

_____

_____

_____

_____

_____

When I **STOPPED** dwelling on the past . . .

I was able to recognize I could appreciate my past, while also moving forward into the future. I struggled for a long time grieving over the events and experiences people that I loved were missing out on; I am grateful to now realize that my future doesn't have to die with people of my past.

—Megan Bigler-Tafolla (35, Florida)

I gave myself permission to forgive myself and move forward. I can't change what happened but I can choose to become better.

—Lucas Webber (33, Minnesota)

I was able to start learning from the things that happened to me. I decided to look at my past as a lesson I could learn from, not a place I needed to stay stuck in.

—Alex Simmons (41, Michigan)

Don't Dwell on the Past

THERE'S NOTHING WRONG with taking a walk down memory lane. It can be fun to reminisce about the past with friends or to look at old photos with family members. If you aren't careful though, a look back at the good old days, might convince you that the best years of your life are behind you.

That's not the only reason why some people dwell on the past, however. You might dwell on the past because something upsetting happened. Someone might have hurt you and you can't forgive them. Or maybe you made a mistake and you can't forgive yourself. You might allow your past experiences to define who you are today and they could have a negative impact on your future.

How Do You Dwell on the Past?

In this chapter, we'll discuss healthy ways to reflect on the past without getting stuck there. We'll also review how a traumatic event might cause your brain to dwell on the past and what you can do about it. And, of course, we'll dive into the exercises that will help you enjoy the present. But first, let's identify the ways in which you get caught up dwelling on the past. Place a checkmark next to the sentences that sound like you.

- ☐ I replay conversations that already happened in my head over and over again (sometimes thinking about all the things I wish I would have said).

- ☐ I spend a lot of time thinking about how to get revenge on people who hurt me in the past.

- ☐ I often think about how different my life might be if I'd only made a few different choices.

- ☐ I beat myself up for my past mistakes.

- ☐ I have a lot of deep regrets that I think about often.

- ☐ I blame my parents and my childhood for many of my problems.

☐ I focus on past happier times in my life to avoid the pain I feel in the present.

☐ I spend a lot of time looking at old photos and reminiscing about the past.

What are some times when you find yourself dwelling on the past?

_____

_____

_____

_____

_____

How do you feel when you're dwelling on the past?

_____

_____

_____

_____

_____

How does dwelling on the past affect your behavior?

_____

_____

_____

_____

_____

Thinking About the Past vs. Dwelling on the Past

There's nothing wrong with thinking about the past. In fact, it can be healthy. You might get a good laugh when you reminisce with your childhood friends. Thinking about the past might also help you learn from your mistakes and gain insight into your behavior.

But constantly replaying awful events in your mind isn't good for your mental health. Rehashing things that cause you to feel bad keeps you stuck in a dark place—whether you're replaying times when you were abused or you're rehashing errors you've made.

Dwelling on the good times too much can be harmful as well. Sometimes people romanticize the past. They only remember the positives in a situation or exaggerate how happy they were when they were in a past relationship. The conclusion that the good times are over prevents them from creating a bright future.

The only time you can change your behavior is in the present. You can't change the past. But you can change right now.

What are some examples of times when you think about the past in a healthy way?

_____

_____

_____

_____

_____

Why I Do It

Whether you can't stop thinking about an event that changed the course of your life or you keep rehashing a conversation you had yesterday, there are many different reasons you might find yourself stuck in the past. Think about the reasons you might dwell on the past and place a checkmark next to the ones that sound familiar. Fill in the blank with any other reasons you can think of that aren't already mentioned in the list.

> I used to replay all the bad choices I made as a way to punish myself. I thought I deserved to keep feeling bad. I learned to remind myself that staying stuck in the past doesn't fix anything. It just keeps me from making better choices in the future.
>
> —Jennifer M. (34, Massachusetts)

- ☐ It helps me avoid the problems I could be tackling right now.
- ☐ It stirs up pleasant feelings.
- ☐ It distracts me from reality.
- ☐ I'm punishing myself for past mistakes.
- ☐ I have past trauma I haven't dealt with.
- ☐ I think dwelling on the past will teach me lessons.
- ☐ It helps me feel connected to people I no longer have contact with.
- ☐ I can't help thinking about the past.
- ☐ _____

Unresolved Trauma

When I talk about not dwelling on the past, I'm not referring to trauma. Traumatic events, like a near-death experience or abuse, get stored in the brain differently. Even though you may go to great lengths to avoid things that remind you of a traumatic event, you might experience flashbacks. Flashbacks are a common symptom of PTSD that involves replaying a painful occurrence. Flashbacks may occur randomly or they may happen when you encounter something that reminds you of the traumatic event—like a certain sound or smell.

If you're dwelling on the past due to unresolved trauma, get professional help. Talk to your doctor, reach out to a therapist, attend a support group, or call a hotline. There are many resources and treatment options available to address traumatic experiences.

Angelina's Story

Angelina walked into my therapy office, sat down in the chair, and said, "Yeah, I'm depressed. But who isn't?" Her physician had recommended she go to therapy to address her depression, but it was clear she didn't really think it was necessary. She did agree to attend a few appointments, but mostly because she wanted to satisfy her physician.

Over the course of several weeks, Angelina shared her story with me. She had a rough childhood and became pregnant when she was nineteen. She had raised her son as a single mom and said, "I wasn't mature enough to have a child until I was about thirty. I wasn't the kind of mom he needed for most of his life."

She dated a lot of men over the years and some of them were abusive. She partied a lot during her twenties and lacked a stable place to live. She and her son moved often and she struggled to keep a steady job.

When Angelina was thirty, she got caught forging a check. Getting arrested made her realize she wanted to turn her life around. She got a steady job, moved into an apartment with her son, and became committed to being the best mom she could be.

Now, at age thirty-five, she had pulled her life together. But she couldn't forgive herself for all the things she had done earlier. Even though her sixteen-year-old son was doing well, she said, "I hate myself for not being a good mom all those years."

Angelina had stopped dating. She also didn't have any friends. She went to work and stayed home. She never did anything fun and she never did anything to take care of herself. And while she chalked this up to the fact that she was a responsible person, it was clear she was also punishing herself for not being the kind of mom she wanted to be earlier.

Over the course of several more weeks, we uncovered the fact that she believed she didn't deserve to have fun. She constantly felt guilty for all the mistakes she'd made and she thought doing something nice for herself now would mean she wasn't really sorry for what she did. She thought she needed to punish herself for her mistakes. It wasn't surprising she felt depressed.

We began to tackle her belief that she had to punish herself. We reviewed how she stayed stuck in the past—by reliving her mistakes constantly in her mind. And we also discussed how her current choices to punish herself might be impacting her son in a negative way.

One of the exercises we worked on was scheduling pleasant activities (something you'll discover later in this chapter). It involved giving herself permission to be kind to herself while also having something to look forward to.

She also learned mindfulness skills (another exercise we'll cover). This helped her practice being present with her son. Rather than perseverating on all the mistakes she'd made in the past, she learned to live in the moment so she could make right now the best moment she could.

Over the course of her treatment, Angelina made incredible progress. Her depression improved once she gave herself permission to stop dwelling on the past. But before she could do that, she had to trust that she wasn't going to heal her old emotional wounds or her son's by punishing herself.

Whether you dwell on something that happened a decade ago or you keep rehashing something that happened in the past hour, here are the exercises I've found most effective for making peace with the past, enjoying the present, and planning for the future.

Change the Channel in Your Brain

You might find that you don't mean to think about the past. A conversation you had last week might just keep replaying in your brain like a movie.

Or you might find your mind constantly drifting back to an ex or rehashing things that happened during your childhood. Dwelling on things you can't change can keep you stuck in a painful place.

You might have tried telling yourself "Just don't think about that" when you want to get your mind off something. If you have, you've likely noticed this isn't very effective. Fortunately, there are some effective ways to change the channel in your brain.

Let's do three quick tasks and I'll show you how changing the channel works. To do this, you're going to need a timer, so you can give yourself thirty seconds to complete each task—grab your phone or a timer before you get started on the tasks below.

1. Spend thirty seconds thinking about white bears. These could be cartoon bears, polar bears, stuffed bears, any kind of white bears. Set the timer and think about all those white bears until your time is out.

2. Now, for the next thirty seconds, think about anything you want. You might think about something that happened yesterday, what you're going to eat for lunch today, or something you're going to do after you're done working on this book. **Just don't think about white bears.**

3. Finally, draw a self-portrait with your nondominant hand in the following box. Do the best you can in thirty seconds.

During the first part of the exercise, were you able to conjure up an image of at least one white bear?

☐ Yes

☐ No

During the second part, did at least one white bear pop into your head when you were trying to avoid thinking about white bears?

☐ Yes

☐ No

During the third part, when you were drawing the picture, did you think about white bears at all?

☐ Yes

☐ No

If you're like most people, you probably didn't have any trouble thinking about white bears during part one. During part two, you likely started thinking about something when a white bear suddenly popped into your mind.

And during part three, you were likely so consumed with the task at hand that the white bears disappeared from your mind altogether.

That's because drawing a picture distracted you. It changed the channel in your brain.

When you find yourself dwelling on the past, take action that changes the channel. You could do something as simple as give yourself an exercise—like drawing a self-portrait with your nondominant hand. But you can likely find better options that will keep you distracted longer. Changing the channel isn't about suppressing thoughts or emotions. It's about preventing yourself from engaging in self-destructive thought patterns or staying stuck in emotions that aren't serving you well.

Some of the best ways to change the channel in your brain involve changing your environment, moving your body, or taxing your brain. Here are some examples of ways in which you could change the channel:

- Organize a closet
- Go for a run
- Listen to a podcast while cleaning the kitchen
- Call a friend to talk about something fun
- Do a crossword puzzle
- Read a book
- Watch a show
- Do some yardwork

How will you know when it's a good idea to change the channel?

_____

_____

_____

_____

_____

What are some things you can do to change the channel in your brain?

_____

_____

_____

_____

_____

Schedule Pleasant Activities

You'll be less likely to dwell on the past when you have something to look forward to. In the therapy office, we often use a strategy called "pleasant activity scheduling." It's good for your mental health to have fun things on your calendar. It doesn't have to be huge things, like a weeklong vacation, that you're looking forward to. While a big thing in the future is good, smaller, more immediate, activities are also important.

The key is to have these things marked on your calendar so you have something to look forward to soon.

It might involve scheduling when you're going to watch your favorite show—even if you're watching it alone. Or it could involve having coffee with your friend on Satur-

> *I used to spend a lot of time wishing I had made different decisions. But I finally realized that a different choice wouldn't have necessarily led to the fairy-tale ending I was imagining. My time is better spent focusing on making positive choices moving forward instead of wishing I had made different choices in the past.*
>
> *—Patricia Grayson (51, Washington, DC)*

day morning. The key is to schedule it a few days in advance so you have something you're happily anticipating.

Then, when you find yourself dwelling on the past, remind yourself of something you have to look forward to in the future.

Here's a sample calendar that has a few pleasant activities someone might be looking forward to.

SUNDAY	MONDAY	TUESDAY	WEDNESDAY	THURSDAY	FRIDAY	SATURDAY
		10 AM Massage				7 PM Dinner w/ Emily
			8 PM Book Club		5 PM Meet Heather at the park	

Now, think about the next two weeks in your calendar. Write down the things you are looking forward to doing. If you don't have several things to put on the calendar, schedule some pleasant activities for yourself right now.

SUNDAY	MONDAY	TUESDAY	WEDNESDAY	THURSDAY	FRIDAY	SATURDAY

> *When I get mad about the things I went through, I remind myself that I can't change the past. But I can choose how I respond to it now. It's up to me to take what happened and create a better life for myself now.*
>
> —Angel Perez, (36, Puerto Rico)

Practice Mindfulness

While some people engage in heavy-duty meditation strategies, you don't have to spend years studying meditation to reap some of the benefits. You can learn to practice mindfulness in just a few minutes a day. Mindfulness involves just being present in the moment, rather than focusing on the past or worrying about the future. Here are some simple ways to practice mindfulness:

1. Pause throughout the day and just notice what you hear, smell, taste, touch, and see. Sometimes we're so lost in thought that we don't even notice the sound of birds chirping or the smell of freshly cut grass.

2. Practice mindfulness with a specific object. Spend a few minutes looking at an ordinary item, like the pattern in your carpet or a paper clip. Observe how it looks. Touch it and notice how it feels. When your thoughts drift to another subject, gently bring them back to the object.

3. Practice mindfulness with a food item. Take a small bite of a piece of chocolate or put a raisin in your mouth. Notice how it feels in your mouth before starting to chew. Pay attention to how it tastes. You might notice things that you never noticed before—like how the texture of a raisin feels on your tongue.

4. Practice mindfulness throughout the day by simply being in the moment. When you're brushing your teeth, pay attention to what you're doing. Or when you're cleaning the kitchen, take a second to notice your surroundings.

It's tempting to multitask. But doing one thing at a time can help you learn to live in the present—which can prevent you from dwelling on the past.

What are some ways in which you can begin to practice mindfulness?

_____

_____

_____

_____

_____

Be more mindful throughout the week. Then, after seven days, see if you notice any differences in how you think, feel, and behave.

Create Your Plan to Stop Dwelling on the Past

What are some things you can do to stop dwelling on the past?

☐ Talk to a professional to help heal unresolved trauma

☐ Forgive myself for a mistake I made

☐ Change the channel in my brain when I'm ruminating

☐ Find ways to make peace with things that happen

☐ Practice mindfulness so I can get used to being in the present

☐ Schedule fun activities in the future so I have things to look forward to

☐ _____

Now let's identify some clear actions you can take to stop dwelling on the past. Taking small steps to heal the pain from the past, enjoy the present, and plan for the future can go a long way toward helping you feel better. Here are some examples of steps you might take to stop dwelling on the past:

➤ I will schedule an appointment with a therapist so I can begin healing from past trauma.

➤ Whenever I start ruminating, I will change the channel in my brain by assigning myself a quick household chore to do.

➤ I will stop rehashing all the things that went wrong in my last relationship with my friends.

➤ When I find myself thinking about how the best days of my life are behind me, I'll focus on scheduling something positive I can do in the future.

➤ When my mom insists on bringing things up from the past over and over again, I'll tell her I don't want to talk about it.

What's one step you can take that will help you stop dwelling on the past?

_____

_____

_____

_____

_____

_____

What will you notice about yourself when you stop dwelling on the past?

_____

_____

_____

_____

_____

How will your life be different?

_____

_____

_____

_____

_____

_____

_____

When I **STOPPED** making the same mistakes over and over . . .

I felt more in control of what lies ahead.

—Vanessa (52, New York)

My life started. I recognized the patterns and I stopped.

—Daisy Lloyd (41, United Kingdom)

I broke free from my pain. I knew my mistakes stemmed from issues in my childhood. But it wasn't until I learned to stop repeating my mistakes that I was really able to move forward.

—Grace Koenig (43, North Carolina)

Don't Make the Same Mistakes Over and Over Again

I CAN'T COUNT how many people have said to me in my therapy office, "I'm never doing that again!" only to come back the next week and say, "I did it again."

We all repeat our mistakes sometimes. That can include anything from relationship blunders to addictions we keep reaching for—even though we don't want to.

Sometimes, we just don't learn from our mistakes. At other times, though, we're so ashamed of our missteps that we just don't see any way out—aside from the unhealthy habit that caused us pain in the first place. Fortunately, there are several things we can do to learn from our mistakes and reduce the likelihood of repeating them.

How Do You Keep Making the Same Mistakes Over and Over Again?

In this chapter, we'll review ways in which you can escape the unhealthy patterns that can cause you to repeat your mistakes and the exercises that will help you learn and do better. First, let's take a look at the ways in which you might repeat your missteps. Place a checkmark next to the statements that sound like you.

☐ I get into unhealthy relationships (friendship or romantic).

☐ I buy things I don't need and later regret it.

☐ I let my emotions dictate my behavior.

☐ I say things when I'm upset that I later regret.

☐ I get into heated arguments even when I know it won't do any good.

☐ I give in to temptations too often.

☐ I turn to the same unhealthy things over and over again to deal with uncomfortable feelings.

Mistakes vs. Repeating the Same Mistakes

Mistakes are an important part of the learning process. If you didn't try new things or push yourself to do things differently, you wouldn't have much of a life. Social mistakes, financial mistakes, emotional mistakes, relationship mistakes, professional mistakes . . . those are just a few of the types of mistakes we can learn from in life. What are some specific mistakes you make over and over again?

- ☐ Eating unhealthy food when I don't want to
- ☐ Staying up later than I plan
- ☐ Putting things off for too long
- ☐ Spending too much time online
- ☐ Sleeping later than I want
- ☐ Buying things I don't need
- ☐ Acting impatient with people
- ☐ Forgetting to do things I say I'm going to do
- ☐ _____

> *For a long time, I was trapped in an endless cycle. My addiction helped me feel better for a minute but I knew it was damaging every part of my life. So many times I said I was going to stop but it didn't last. I wasn't able to break free until I asked for help getting out. Only then could I stop repeating my mistakes.*
>
> Jean L. (39, Florida)

Why Do You Repeat Your Mistakes?

Some mistakes serve a purpose. You might scarf down a giant bag of chips when you're having a bad day because eating helps you feel better for a minute. Or, you might jump from one bad relationship to another because being with someone feels better than being alone—at least temporarily. After all, you wouldn't repeat your mistakes unless you were gaining something from them.

There may be different reasons you repeat certain mistakes. Think of the mistakes you've repeated. Place a checkmark next to the reasons that likely drove your behavior. If you can think of any other reasons that aren't on the list, write them down on the blank line.

☐ I convince myself things will be different this time.

☐ I tell myself I just need to do whatever I can to get through the day.

☐ I didn't learn from the mistake the first time.

☐ I don't think I'm capable of doing any better.

☐ I don't think I deserve better.

☐ I don't know what else to do.

☐ I struggle to resist temptation.

☐ It's easier to just keep doing the same thing over and over again.

☐ I have an addiction.

☐ I set my goals impossibly high.

☐ I just don't think I'm good enough to do better.

☐ _____

Think of 3 mistakes you've repeated:

1. _____

2. _____

3. _____

Now consider the reason(s) you repeated each one:

1. _____

2. _____

3. _____

Becky's physician recommended she seek therapy because she struggled to stick to her health goals. Becky's blood pressure had slowly crept up over the years. Her physician had warned her several times that if she didn't make changes to her lifestyle, she would need to start taking medication.

Every time she received that warning, she set out to make some changes. She started eating healthier. She got more exercise. She drank less. She even stopped drinking coffee.

But it never lasted for more than a week or two. She'd end up right back where she was before—or maybe even worse.

During our appointments, she would tell me, "I go for a whole week on a low-sodium diet without any processed food. But then I go wild the second I can. I'll have one Friday night where I'll eat pizza and chips and drink beer and then I think since I've gone off course anyway, I might as well treat myself all weekend." By the time Monday rolled around, she'd convince herself she was a failure and there wasn't much sense in trying again.

She said she thought she was motivated to change sometimes but that motivation didn't seem to last. She worried about her health quite a bit. She had several relatives who had struggled with health issues, including heart attacks and strokes. She didn't want to increase her health risks. She had moments though where she didn't seem to care, and it was as if her brain was working against her.

At times, she didn't believe she was capable of change. "I am not the kind of person who can just act healthy," she said. "I don't have enough willpower to say no to pizza and I don't have enough motivation to say yes to working out."

Those sentences made it clear why she was struggling so much. She believed she couldn't be a healthy person and whenever she did something that she perceived to be unhealthy, it reinforced her belief that she was incapable of making a change. She kept making the same mistakes over and over again because she blamed herself for being inadequate.

Our work together focused on strategies that could change her beliefs. She had to see that it was all about the choices she made and mistakes weren't evidence of a character flaw.

Slowly, over time, she grew to see that she wasn't either completely healthy or completely unhealthy. Like everyone, she would make some healthy choices and some not-so-healthy choices. Each time she made an unhealthy choice, she had a decision to make—what was she going to do next? She could either beat herself up for messing up and convince herself there was no point in changing, or she could learn from her mistake and take that knowledge to do better. One of the most helpful exercises she did involved learning how to reframe her shame (something we'll cover in the exercise section).

To her surprise, harsh self-criticism wasn't the answer to making lasting change. Self-compassion was. Once she learned how to forgive herself for a misstep, she was free to do better. By the end of her treatment she was able to recover from her mistakes much better and she felt confident she could work toward reaching her goals even though she would have rough times.

Mental Strength Exercises

Don't allow yourself to become convinced that you're beyond help. There are many steps you can take to create lasting change that will prevent you from repeating your mistakes. Here are some of my favorite strategies and exercises for taking responsibility, creating change, and interrupting the cycle of repeated mistakes.

Own Your Mistakes

Before you can avoid repeating a mistake, you have to acknowledge that you made one in the first place. You might find there are times, though, when it's tempting to blame other people. Maybe you said something rude and upset someone. Rather than taking ownership, it may be easier to say "You're too sensitive" rather than "I was wrong."

> *I speak with my friends about my mistakes.*
>
> —Claudia Cristea
> (46, Romania)

If you're not careful, you might even end up investing more energy in covering up mistakes, hiding them, or excusing them than addressing them.

This often stems from our desire to avoid getting into trouble or looking bad. If you accidentally broke the coffee maker at work, it's easier to quickly walk away than to tell someone it needs repair. Or if you forgot to pay a bill on time, you might be tempted to hide it from your partner who is going to be upset that you weren't "responsible" enough to pay on time.

It's important to own your mistakes. And it can be quite freeing to do so—although scary at first.

It's also important to recognize that just because something isn't your fault, doesn't mean it's not your responsibility. Your genetics may be partially to blame for a drinking problem. But it's still your responsibility to address it. If your unhealthy habits are rooted in your childhood trauma, it's not your fault. But your habits are still your responsibility to address.

The first person you need to admit the mistake to is yourself. You might be tempted to make an excuse that blames someone else. But owning your mistake—and taking full responsibility—is crucial.

Then you can acknowledge to someone else that you made the mistake. You might need to tell your boss you missed a deadline. Or you might need to tell your partner that you spent more money than you had agreed upon. Coming clean to people who are directly affected by your mistake is essential.

You might also find it freeing to acknowledge your mistakes to people who aren't directly affected. For example, you might tell your friends about a mistake you made at work. Or you might tell your family about your latest social blunder. Talking about your mistakes can ensure that you don't feel like you need to keep up a charade that you're perfect. When you start sharing your mistakes, other people will likely start sharing their mistakes too. Over time, talking about inevitable missteps feels more comfortable, and you'll experience less pressure to present yourself as perfect.

What is a time when you made a mistake but struggled to own it?

_____

_____

_____

_____

_____

Why is it sometimes hard to take responsibility for your mistakes?

_____

_____

_____

_____

_____

What steps could you have taken to own your mistake?

_____

_____

_____

_____

_____

How can you own your mistakes even when it's tough to do so?

_____

_____

_____

_____

_____

Reframe Your Shame

Guilt is helpful. But shame isn't. Shame can keep you stuck in a cycle where you're more likely to repeat your mistakes.

Here's the difference:

Guilt: I made a bad choice.

Shame: I'm a bad person.

When you catch yourself being too hard on yourself for a mistake you made, it's important to reframe your shame.

When you think, "I'm an idiot for messing up," remind yourself, "I made a mistake. I can learn and move forward."

What's a time when you shamed yourself for messing up?

_____

_____

_____

_____

_____

What kind of things did you think?

_____

_____

_____

_____

_____

What could you have told yourself instead?

_____

_____

_____

_____

_____

Call Yourself by Name

Pause for a second and think about what you call yourself inside your own head. Do you say, "I have to get up now," or "You have to get up now?" Or do you call yourself by name, "OK, Susan, time to get up now."

Maybe you do a variety of those things.

But there's some evidence that indicates you might want to start calling yourself by name. When you say, "Brenda, you can do this," or "Rob, take a deep breath and do your best," you might actually do better.

It's a sports psychology trick adopted by many elite athletes because there's evidence that calling yourself by name calms you down and helps you perform better.

So when you make a mistake, speak to yourself calmly and compassionately and call yourself by name. It might help you stay in the moment so you can learn from your mistake and move forward.

What's an example of a time when it may be helpful for you to call yourself by name?

_____

_____

_____

_____

_____

What can you tell yourself?

_____

_____

_____

_____

_____

Act Like the Person You Want to Become

You might have found yourself accepting certain things about yourself as a way to justify repeat mistakes. You may declare, "Well, I am just the kind of person who speaks their mind," as a way to justify hurting someone's feelings. Or you might conclude, "I'm a shy person so I just won't say anything in meetings."

But changing your behavior will change everything. If you want to be a kinder person, act kind now. If you want to be a more outgoing person, start being more outgoing.

Changing your behavior shifts the way you see yourself. It also shifts the way you feel.

This can be critical when it comes to overcoming mistakes. Decide who you want to be and start acting like that person now.

What kind of person do you want to become? Kind, healthy, happy, friendly, etc.?

_____

_____

_____

_____

_____

What can you start doing today to begin acting like that person?

_____

_____

_____

_____

_____

Think of a common mistake you repeat. How could acting like the person you want to be prevent you from making that mistake again?

_____

_____

_____

_____

_____

> I used to just tell myself, "Don't make that mistake again." But I usually did. Now I look ahead and figure out how to help myself be more successful. A little planning helps me do better the next time.
>
> —Kaley N. (38, Montana)

Set Yourself up for Success

One reason you might keep repeating your mistakes is that you're setting yourself up for failure. You may need to modify your environment or make some changes in your life so you can be successful.

If you're trying to stick to healthy snacks in the afternoon, don't keep chocolates on your desk. If you want to increase the likelihood that you'll go for a walk before work, get your clothes and your sneakers ready the night before.

You can even put some obstacles in the way. For example, if you are going to keep cookies in the house, keep them on the highest shelf in the back. Or put them in the closet in your spare room so they are out of sight.

When you make a mistake, take a minute and think about how you can avoid making it again. What changes can you make to your schedule, your behavior, or your environment to increase the chances that you'll succeed next time?

How can you set yourself up for success to avoid repeating a specific mistake?

_____

_____

_____

_____

_____

Is there an obstacle you can introduce that will make one of your unhealthy habits tougher to access?

_____

_____

_____

_____

_____

Take a minute to think about what kind of person you want to be this week. Do you want to be happy, friendly, generous, empathetic, or something else? Every day, do at least one thing that helps you act like that kind of person. By the end of the week, you'll see it becomes easier to act like the person you want to become.

Create Your Plan to Stop Repeating Your Mistakes

What are some things you can do to stop repeating your mistakes?

☐ Start acknowledging the mistakes I make

☐ Stop shaming myself when I mess up

☐ Set myself up for success

☐ Consider whether I'm really ready to make a change

☐ Take time to learn from my mistake before trying again

☐ Call myself by name as I move forward

☐ Act like the person I want to become

☐ _____

Now take a minute to identify some clear action steps you can take to stop repeating a mistake. Small steps can help you learn and grow from your mistakes so you don't stay stuck repeating them. Here are some small steps you might take to stop repeating a specific mistake:

➤ I will schedule an appointment with an addiction medicine specialist to help me stay sober this time.

➤ I will take responsibility for my share of the relationship problems so I can focus on improving myself moving forward.

➤ I will take time to sharpen my interview skills before applying for more jobs.

➤ I am going to sign up for an anger management class so I don't keep losing my temper.

➤ I am going to find twenty minutes every day to do some physical activity. If I miss a day, I will not shame myself but instead, I will work on getting back on track the next day.

What's one step you can take that will help you stop repeating your mistakes?

_____

_____

_____

_____

_____

What will you notice about yourself once you stop repeating your mistakes?

_____

_____

_____

_____

_____

How will your life be different?

_____

_____

_____

_____

_____

_____

When I **STOPPED** resenting other people's success . . .

I realized that every single one of us is completely different and has different strengths and weaknesses. Your strength might be someone else's weakness or vice versa. Therefore, it's not fair to yourself or others to be resentful.

—Amy Brooks (40, South Carolina)

When I stopped resenting other people's success I started to have a better life.

—Clovis Ximenes De Melo Junior (61, Brazil)

I started listening to people without judging whether they deserved success. I could be happy for them when good things happened without feeling like it was my job to determine if they were worthy of having good things happen to them.

—Dawn Garrison (29, Florida)

Don't
Resent
Other
People's
Success

WE USED TO compare our success with the people who were physically around us. "Keeping up with the Joneses" involved trying to keep up with the people in your neighborhood—at least when the term was coined.

Nowadays, you might find yourself looking at successful people everywhere on the internet. Whether you're seeing your former classmates posting about their luxury vacations on social media or you're gaining a glimpse inside your boss's mansion during Zoom meetings, it's tough not to resent people when you're seeing their highlight reels on your screen all day long. Resenting other people's success can take a serious toll on your well-being. Ironically, it can even reduce your chances of becoming successful.

How Do You Resent Other People's Success?

In this chapter, we'll examine how to recognize when you're resenting other people's success and the steps you can take to stop doing it. First, though, let's take a closer look at the ways in which you might be feeling this resentment. Read the following statements and place a checkmark next to the ones that sound like you.

☐ I scroll through social media feeling angry about people who look happy.

☐ I dislike people who are more attractive or have more money than me.

☐ I think about why certain people don't deserve their good fortune.

☐ I put people down behind their backs.

☐ I often wish bad things would happen to certain people.

☐ I feel bad when I'm around people who have what I want.

☐ I think other people are "ahead" of me in life in some way.

What's an example of a time when you've resented someone else's success?

_____

_____

_____

_____

_____

What kind of thoughts did you have during that time?

_____

_____

_____

_____

_____

How did your resentment affect your behavior?

_____

_____

_____

_____

_____

Admiring Someone vs. Resenting Them

You can admire someone for their achievements, natural talents, and good fortune. You may still have moments when you question how they got to be so "lucky." But overall, admiration provides an opportunity to learn from others.

Resentment, on the other hand, distracts you from your goals. It involves not wanting someone to have good things in their life. You might wish your sister wasn't so beautiful or you might secretly wish your friend would get fired from their high-paying job.

You might convince yourself that there are only so many good looks, so much wealth, and so much happiness to go around. And when people have those things, you might conclude they're taking it away from you. It's really about a scarcity mindset.

Feelings of resentment can lead to unhealthy behaviors that can decrease your happiness and reduce your chances of success. You might speak ill of that wealthy friend you resent or you might even try to secretly sabotage that coworker you didn't think deserved a promotion. Before we talk about resentment, let's look at healthy admiration.

Who are some people you admire, and what can you learn from them?

1. _____

2. _____

3. _____

Why Do You Resent Successful People?

You might just have one area of your life where you grow resentful. It often stems from insecurity—like about how you look or how much money you earn. But it's important to take time to examine why you feel the way you do and when it happens. Think about the times you've resented people and the reasons you felt that way. It can be tough to acknowledge these not-so-nice parts about ourselves, but it's important to understand why it happens. Place a checkmark next to the statements that sound familiar and fill in the blank with anything you can think of that didn't make the list.

☐ I don't really know what I want out of life.

☐ I feel bad about myself.

☐ I think undeserving people always win out in the end.

☐ I don't know how to define success.

☐ I think successful people are taking away my opportunities to succeed.

☐ I think I was born unlucky or misfortunate.

☐ _____

Who is someone you have resented and what specifically did you resent about them?

_____

_____

_____

_____

_____

What can you learn about yourself based on the people you feel resentment toward or the times when you feel resentful?

_____

_____

_____

_____

_____

I grew up in poverty—in and out of shelters and on the streets. I was severely abused and placed into foster care at age eleven. I never returned to my biological parents due to the extent of the abuse. I've worked very hard for the degree I earned, home I live in, and beautiful family I've made. I don't resent anyone who has what I don't. I have treasures beyond possessions—a healed heart, children who are growing up in a home of love and nurturing and generational cycles that have been broken because I made hard choices in my life.

—Jessica Aikens (40, Maine)

Jon's Story

Jon walked into my therapy office saying he wasn't as successful as he could be, and he wanted to uncover whatever issues were likely holding him back in life. But whenever he began talking about the things going on in his life, the conversation always drifted to all the things going on in everyone else's life.

He and his wife earned less money than everyone else in their social group. Some of their friends got to do some fairly glamorous things, like travel around the country and attend important-sounding meetings.

Hearing about his friends' newest purchases or their upcoming travel plans caused him to feel a little resentful. He thought he was smarter, more capable, and more competent than most of them. The more successful his friends became, the less he enjoyed spending time with them. He knew that he'd started showing his irritation when they got together.

We decided to create Jon's definition of success (an exercise you'll do a little later). When he was done, Jon had a solid picture of what a successful life looked like to him—he wanted to raise nice children who worked hard. He wanted to be involved in their lives by attending their after-school activities and he wanted to be able to help them with their homework. When he began thinking about how important it was to him to be a good husband and a good father, he viewed his friends' lives a little differently.

Rather than feeling frustrated by the fact that his friends could afford to hire people to do their home-improvement projects, he reminded himself that doing the work himself gave him an opportunity to teach his kids new skills. They spent quality time together as he repaired broken tiles or fixed a clogged drain.

Once he was able to start focusing on his own definition of success, he stopped resenting his friends who were working toward their own definition of success. He no longer viewed them as his competition.

At his last therapy session he said, "It's so easy to forget what's important in life, especially nowadays. But giving my kids more time and attention is what matters to me most right now."

Mental Strength Exercises

If you find yourself resenting other people's success, you might think the solution is for you to step up your game in life. But the truth is, no matter how great you are doing, there will always be someone who is wealthier, happier, and more attractive. So the antidote involves changing your mindset. Here are some great exercises for putting an end to resenting other people's success.

> *You remind yourself everyone has their struggles and you may not see them. Also, I remember what's happened to me and what I have or have not gotten has made me more interesting and made me me.*
>
> —Erin Mantz (51, Maryland)

Make an Inside/Outside Shoebox

When I see therapy clients who resent other people for having what they want, I sometimes assign them the inside/outside shoebox exercise. Some people actually do the project—an art project of sorts. Other people (who aren't really into that sort of thing), talk about how their shoebox would look if they made one.

Here's the exercise:

Get a shoebox or other small box and some old magazines.

Cut out pictures from the magazines (you can also make your own pictures to cut out) that represent what other people see when they look at you. You might include things like your hobbies or things you're known for—like those chocolate chip cookies you bake or the red car you drive. Place the pictures on the outside of the box.

What would those things on the outside of the box remind other people about you?

_____

_____

_____

_____

_____

Are there any people in your life who would be surprised by any of the things on the outside of your box? Maybe your coworkers don't know about your hobbies or maybe your grandmother has no idea how well-respected you are in the business world.

_____

_____

_____

_____

_____

Now, decorate the inside of the shoebox to represent what you're really like on the inside. You might include words that describe thoughts and feelings or pictures that depict how you see yourself.

Would your friends and family be surprised to see the inside of your box or do you think they'd know those things about you?

_____

_____

_____

_____

_____

Most people tell me that even their friends, family members, and even their partners would be surprised to see the inside of their box.

We all have things we don't share with others—even those closest to us. It might be something about your past or it could be ongoing struggles you have. But everyone has some secrets and some things they keep private.

When we look at successful people, we forget that we're just looking at the outside of their shoe-boxes. We have no idea what's on the inside.

As a therapist, I get to hear how people feel. Patients often tell me things they've never told anyone else. And we work on problems that aren't evident on the outside. I know that people who look like they have it all together on the outside are also fighting secret battles on the inside.

Think of someone whose success you have resented. What are some of the struggles they might be experiencing that you don't see?

_____

_____

_____

_____

_____

> *I remind myself that a core value of mine is "win-win" and that their success does not limit my success or how I define it. I recently learned that resentment is in the envy family of feelings—so I am changing my thinking to ask what I am really envying when I start feeling resentful.*
>
> —Amy Jurgensen (41, Michigan)

Create Your Own Definition of Success

What's your definition of success in life?

_____

_____

_____

_____

_____

If you had trouble identifying a clear definition, you're not alone. It's hard to know sometimes what it means to be successful. Do you need to be rich? Happy? Have a big family? Own a home? Move to a city? Make a contribution to society?

Society places a lot of value on external things, like your income and your job title. But that doesn't mean you really believe those things make someone successful.

It's hard though sometimes to identify a definition of success looking forward. You might find it's helpful to look back. This can help you gain a little perspective.

Imagine you are one hundred years old and you're thinking about the life you had. What would make you think you'd lived a great life?

_____

_____

_____

_____

_____

Now imagine a good friend is introducing you to someone new. They give a brief description of who you are to that other person. How would you hope to be described?

_____

_____

_____

_____

_____

Now that you've identified that, what is your definition of success? Keep this definition handy and refer to it whenever you're tempted to resent someone else for working toward their definition of success.

_____

_____

_____

_____

_____

Look at Other People as Opinion Holders, Not Competitors

In *13 Things Mentally Strong Women Don't Do*, I talk about the dangers of social comparisons. Upward social comparisons, like thinking someone is more attractive or richer than you, fuel envy and resentment. On the flipside, downward social comparisons, like assuming someone is less intelligent or less motivated than you can lead to pity (which isn't good for your mental health or your relationship).

Rather than thinking of someone else as your competitor, look at them as an opinion holder. Then you'll see that you can learn from people. And you'll recognize that their knowledge or skills don't diminish you.

Here's the difference:

Competitive thought: She's a better businessperson than I am.

Opinion-holder thought: I could learn new skills by watching how she conducts business.

What's a competitive thought you have about someone?

_____

_____

_____

_____

_____

_____

What's a thought you can replace it with to remind yourself that the person is an opinion holder?

_____

_____

_____

_____

_____

Cheer Other People On

Don't wait until you feel genuine excitement for someone to cheer them on. You can congratulate people and say kind things even when you are feeling a little jealous.

That's not to say you should act "fake." But cheering other people on can stir up happy feelings even if you aren't feeling them at first.

Get into the habit of being kind and congratulating people. You might start by cheering on strangers on social media. Leave a kind comment on LinkedIn. Or reach out to someone whose work you appreciate.

If you read an article you enjoy, tell the author of the piece what you liked about it. Tell a musician that you like their music. Or leave a positive review for a business that you think is doing a good job.

Make it a daily habit to cheer people on and over time, it can become second nature. Putting good vibes out in the world feels good. And when you feel better, you'll likely feel happier when people you actually know are succeeding too.

What are some steps you can take to cheer on other people in your life?

_____

_____

_____

_____

_____

_____

A WORD OF CAUTION ABOUT CHEERING SOMEONE ON

If someone says they feel nervous about an upcoming interview, saying something like, "Oh don't worry about it! You'll do just fine," isn't cheering them on. A statement like that minimizes their feelings. Instead, it can be more supportive to say, "I'll be rooting for you!"

Pay attention to your social media use. Does social media cause you to feel resentment? Do you find yourself thinking about how other people aren't deserving of the things they have? Do you feel like you aren't good enough when you're using social media?

Consider the people and the accounts you follow. It's important that social media helps bolster your goals and values, not distract you from what's most important in life. Don't fill your time listening to and watching other people brag about how great their lives are if it causes you to experience resentment. Follow people who inspire you. Set yourself up for success by muting, unfollowing, and deleting as needed.

Create Your Plan to Stop Resenting Other People's Success

What are some things you can do to stop resenting other people's success?

☐ Limit my time on social media and be conscious of who I follow

☐ Cheer people on

☐ Stay focused on my own definition of success

☐ Keep other people's lives in proper perspective (remember they may not be as "perfect" as they look from the outside)

☐ Look at other people as opinion holders, not my competitors

☐ _____

Now work on identifying a concrete action step you can take to stop resenting someone else's success. Here are a few examples of steps you might take to feel less threatened by anyone else's success:

➤ I will stop looking at social media profiles that cause me to think everyone else's life is perfect.

➤ I will spend time with my friend who is supportive of me, and I will genuinely cheer my friend on regularly.

➤ Whenever my parents remind me how well my siblings are doing, I will remind myself that they have different goals in life than I do and I can be happy living with less.

➤ I will stop attending conferences that encourage me to make my self-worth contingent on achievement only.

What's one step you can take to stop resenting other people's success?

_____

_____

_____

_____

_____

_____

What will you notice about yourself once you stop resenting other people's success?

_____

_____

_____

_____

_____

_____

How will your life be different?

_____

_____

_____

_____

_____

_____

When I **STOPPED** giving up after my first failure . . .

I saw I didn't need to be embarrassed if I failed once. I should be proud I was willing to try twice.

—Christy Bennett (35, Canada)

I knew how much I had been missing out on. Almost no one succeeds the first time they try to do something really big.

—Whitney Cramer (42, South Carolina)

I started cutting myself some slack. I realized there was no reason why I had to get everything right the first time. And if I did, life might be kind of boring.

—Christopher D. (48, Australia)

Don't
Give Up
After Your
First Failure

I OFTEN GIVE keynote speeches at conferences and to private companies about how to avoid the traps that rob us of mental strength. Whenever I mention our tendency to give up after our first failure, I'll see a lot of people nodding their heads as if they understand failure is part of the process. That's not surprising because audiences are often comprised of successful, career-driven individuals who have likely failed a few times along the way.

But after my talks, many of those same people who were nodding their heads in agreement will come up to me afterward and discuss a failure that stopped them in their tracks outside the office. Like the man who told me he had wanted to be an entrepreneur. But after his first business venture failed, he thought it was safer to go work for someone else's company. Or the woman who said she once auditioned for a TEDx talk, but didn't get selected. She said she admired public speakers but clearly, she wasn't cut out for it.

Like many of us, these individuals could tolerate failure in certain areas of their lives, but not others. And it only took one failure to stop them from trying certain things again.

How Do You Give Up After Your First Failure?

In this chapter, we're going to cover why we sometimes give up after failure and the exercises that can help us keep going after we've failed. But first, let's look at the ways in which you might be giving up after your first failure. Take a look at the following statements and place a checkmark next to the ones that sound like you.

☐ If something doesn't work out the first time, I assume I wasn't meant to do it.

☐ When I can't do a task well, I give it to someone else.

☐ If I'm not good at something right away, I decide I can't ever be good at it.

☐ I make excuses for failure so I don't take the blame.

☐ If I fail, I pretend I didn't really care if I succeeded anyway.

☐ When I fail, I feel too embarrassed to try again.

☐ I don't tell anyone when I fail.

☐ I lose interest fast if it doesn't look like I will succeed the first time.

What's an example of a time when you gave up after your first failure?

_____

_____

_____

_____

_____

How did you feel?

_____

_____

_____

_____

_____

What kinds of thoughts were running through your head?

_____

_____

_____

_____

_____

Quitting vs. Giving Up Because You Failed

Quite often, I hear people say things like "Never quit." I completely disagree. We should quit lots of things. And I'm not just talking about bad habits, like smoking.

It's OK to quit something that isn't serving you well. If you don't like your job, there's no glory in suffering through for another decade. Quit and find another one if you want.

If you start a second job in an attempt to pay down your debt and realize that you feel completely miserable as you try to work eighty hours per week, quit!

Life is too short to keep doing things you hate. If you fail at something that wasn't for you, you don't have to try again.

But if something is really worth it to you, don't let those uncomfortable emotions that accompany failure talk you out of trying again. You might be embarrassed, disappointed, and scared. That's OK. Keep going if you still want to reach your goal.

What is a time in your life when you quit after a failure and you're glad you quit?

_____

_____

_____

_____

_____

What's a time when you gave up after failure and you wish you had tried again?

_____

_____

_____

_____

_____

Why Do You Give Up After Failure?

Every failure is an opportunity to make a decision. Do you give up or do you try again? Take a few minutes to consider why you sometimes allow failure to keep you from trying again.

☐ I'm embarrassed.

☐ I feel too frustrated to keep going.

☐ I think I'm a loser who can't do any better.

☐ I'm afraid people will make fun of me.

☐ I'm afraid I won't be able to handle it if I fail again.

☐ _____

Sometimes our decision to avoid trying again is less about the failure itself and more about our fear that others will judge us for failing.

Are you more bothered by failure or by people seeing you fail?

_____

_____

_____

_____

_____

> *The biggest failure I have felt was after grad school, not getting a job I thought would easily be mine. I wasn't even a finalist. My heart was broken. I did a lot of soul-searching, talked to a therapist, and was in a low point for a few months. I worked to feel better, find solutions, and eventually a better opportunity arose that worked out better than the original job. Since then I have always known things are temporary.*
>
> *—Heidi Smith (40, Minnesota)*

Nate started therapy because he wanted to address some unresolved childhood issues. He was raised by a single mom who had a substance abuse problem and his father rarely had any contact with him.

He wanted help overcoming fears that he wasn't good enough. He was certain that issue stemmed from the fact that many of his mother's boyfriends had been abusive toward him growing up.

One of the areas where Nate lacked confidence was in his physical abilities. He said, "I didn't have any siblings to play with and no one ever played ball with me. I spent my entire childhood watching TV. I didn't even learn how to ride a bicycle until I was an adult."

Despite feeling unathletic, he'd been going to the gym for years. And with some encouragement from a friend, he had decided to complete a triathlon. He trained hard for a couple of months and was proud of the work he put in to get ready.

But the race didn't go as planned. He'd trained in the gym. Running and biking on the road felt completely different. And he'd trained for the swimming portion of the race almost exclusively in a pool. Swimming in a river was much more difficult. The currents and the waves exhausted him and he didn't finish the race.

At his first appointment after the race, he said, "I had no business attempting a race like that. I embarrassed myself by trying." The old tapes in his head about not being good enough were playing in full force.

We discussed his options. Of course, he could decide that he didn't want to try another race. Or he could try again. Initially, he wanted to quit. We explored the reasons he wanted to quit (something you'll explore a little later in this chapter). He concluded he wanted to quit because he was terrified he'd fail again. He wasn't sure he could handle another failed race. He said, "I already feel like a failure. I don't need more proof I'm a loser."

We spent some time talking about stories of successful athletes who failed many times along the way. We also reviewed times when his other failures had turned into great comebacks—like the time he didn't get one job only to be offered a much better job later.

Over the course of several weeks, Nate decided to train for another triathlon. This time, he'd know what to expect and he could incorporate that knowledge into his regimen.

As he trained for his next race, one of the things we talked about was how giving up after his first failure (something he usually did) reinforced his belief that he wasn't good enough. Challenging that belief by trying again helped him see that he was more capable than he gave himself credit for. Trying again also reminded him that he had choices—he could choose to stop trying at some point or he could choose to try again. But he didn't have to automatically give up if he failed once. We also challenged his belief that he wasn't an athletic person. He could work on increasing his athleticism if he wanted to. Holding on to that old belief that he couldn't be athletic wasn't in line with his goal to complete a triathlon.

Nate competed in another triathlon later that year. He didn't win, but he finished the race. He was satisfied that he had tried again but he realized that the title "triathlon finisher" didn't erase his insecurities as he'd hoped. He still needed to do some work in therapy to address his unhealed emotional wounds. As we neared the end of his treatment he said, "I now see that one accomplishment won't ever make me finally feel 'good enough.' But knowing that I can handle failure and try again chips away at my belief that I'm destined to be a loser."

Mental Strength Exercises

It's scary to try again after you've failed once. After all, there's no guarantee that your next attempt will be successful. But these mental strength exercises can help you find the courage to try again—and to do so with more knowledge than you had before.

How to Know When to Quit

While perseverance through tough times is important, refusing to quit isn't always a sign of strength. And choosing to quit doesn't mean you're a failure.

There are plenty of times when it makes sense to quit. And sometimes, it takes a fair amount of strength to walk away.

Here are five times when you should quit something:

1. You discover the risks outweigh the potential rewards.

Let's say you decide you're going to run a marathon. As part of your training, you're going to complete a 5K race. You fail to finish the race because you're so out of breath. You see your doctor and discover you have an underlying heart condition and training for a marathon right now would put too much of a strain on your heart. Your doctor advises you to stop training for the marathon, as doing so might put your health at serious risk.

The risk clearly outweighs the reward. Although the medal or T-shirt you might get for crossing the finish line would be cool, putting your health (and your life) at risk aren't worth the bragging rights.

Giving up your goal would be wise, not weak.

If at any point you decide that trying again after you fail is going to cost you your health, your relationships, or your peace of mind, quitting might be your best option.

What's an example of a time when you quit something because the risks outweighed the potential rewards?

_____

_____

_____

_____

_____

2. The reward isn't worth the effort.

Failure might teach you that the reward you're striving for just isn't enough to justify the effort it will take to keep going.

The problem might be that you overestimated the reward. For example, you might have assumed earning 10 percent more or losing ten pounds would somehow make your life 100 percent better.

As you begin working on trying to make those things happen, you might realize that success isn't going to deliver the giant reward you'd been dreaming about. You might decide not to invest the time and effort it would take to receive the payoff.

What's an example of a time when you quit something because the reward wasn't worth the effort?

_____

_____

_____

_____

_____

3. Your goals have changed.

Let's say you decide to launch your own business. So far, though, your efforts to turn your little side hustle into a full-blown gig have failed. Your goal to launch your business might take a backseat the second you find out you have a health problem. You might then decide to keep your current job (and the awesome health insurance coverage) and focus on your health before applying for another position.

The first time you fail at something also might teach you that you don't really want to pursue a goal. Whether it's because things around you have changed or you've changed, abandoning your goals might make sense.

What's an example of a time when you quit something because your goals changed?

_____

_____

_____

_____

4. *The process doesn't align with your values.*

While paying off your debt in five years might sound like an honorable goal, the work it will take to make it happen might not align with your values. If you value time with your family, working three jobs to pay off your bills isn't a good idea.

After a few months, you might decide your goal is at odds with your values. And you might choose to walk away.

What's an example of a time when you quit because the process didn't align with your values?

_____

_____

_____

_____

5. *You've dug yourself into a deep hole.*

In psychology, we refer to this as the "sunk-cost fallacy." It's the notion that once we've invested a lot of time or money into something, we should keep going—even if it's not likely to be successful.

For example, if your new business is losing money every month, you might be tempted to keep going until you can earn that money back. Similarly, you might want to finish a project that you've devoted endless hours to even though it's not working out, simply because you don't want the time you've put in so far to be wasted.

It's tough to walk away from something you've worked hard on. But it's not rational to keep going just because you've invested a lot of time or money getting yourself into a mess. Instead, you should quit before you dig yourself into an even deeper hole.

What's an example of a time when you quit after you dug yourself into a deep hole?

_____

_____

_____

_____

_____

Study Famous Failures

When we look at success stories, we often are only looking at the end. We see successful inventors, entrepreneurs, and celebrities who are thriving. What we don't see are the failures that got them there.

The more we look at just the end result, the more we assume people's path to success was probably a smooth one. And that assumption can interfere with our ability to risk failure in our own lives.

This is true with students. A 2016 study, "Even Einstein Struggled: Effects of Learning about Great Scientists' Struggles on High School Students' Motivation to Learn Science," published in the *Journal of Educational Psychology* demonstrates how important it is to teach kids about failure. Researchers found that when high school teachers taught science students about the successful feats of famous inventors, scientists, and engineers, the stu-

> Sometimes I feel like I'm in the gutter, worthless. That's the time you have to sometimes put one foot in front of the other just to generate momentum. I try to post motivational quotes and things in my home so that when I least feel it, I am reminded of values I know to be important and true.
>
> —Scott (53, Texas)

dents' grades actually declined. When the teachers started sharing stories about the failures these successful individuals endured prior to becoming successful, the students' grades went up.

While it's great to know that Edison created the lightbulb, knowing how many of his inventions failed can be even more powerful. Students who learned about failure felt better about taking risks. They also realized that failure didn't have to be the end of the road.

Just like the students, learning about famous failures might help you take more risks. You might put yourself out there, dare to fail, and become motivated to try again.

What are some of your favorite stories of famous people who failed? If you don't know many, look up famous failures and you'll find some interesting stories.

_____

_____

_____

_____

_____

Recall Your Own Comeback Stories

While I used to think I had a collection of failures that I never wanted to recount again, over the years, I've grown to realize that some of my biggest failures were opportunities for my biggest comebacks.

I got rejected by two different graduate schools. I remember ripping up the letters and throwing them in the trash and not wanting to tell anyone I'd received them. Fortunately, the third school I applied to let me in and I went on to get my degree. But about ten years after receiving those letters, a woman came up to me after hearing me give a talk on mental strength. She asked me to sign a copy of _13 Things Mentally Strong People Don't Do_ and said she couldn't wait to tell her fellow students she heard me speak. I asked her which college she was attending and she named one of the colleges that rejected me. The same school that wouldn't let me in now has my book on their list of recommended reading. That's my favorite personal comeback story.

Those stories—coupled with lots of other stories of times I failed—drive me to do better. But not because I want to say to people who rejected me, "I'll show you!" It's because those stories remind me that I can keep trying for myself after I fail. I do it for me though, not to prove anyone wrong.

Thinking back about how awful I felt, how I found the courage to try again, and how I felt after I tried, reminds me that I can use failure as an opportunity to grow stronger and get better.

Write your own comeback story below. You don't necessarily need a huge failure to enjoy a good comeback. Maybe you got turned down for a job but found a better one. Or maybe, right after you got rejected by one love interest, you found someone amazing. Include details about how you found the courage to try again. Whenever you are tempted to give up, remind yourself of your story.

_____

_____

_____

_____

_____

> *I used to worry about what other people were going to think of me if I failed at something. Now I just look at failure as an opportunity to show people what I'm really made of. I'm someone who isn't afraid to keep trying after I fail once.*
>
> —Jeff Veilleux (45, France)

Talk to Yourself Like a Trusted Friend

If your friend called to say, "I didn't get the job," you'd probably offer some kind words of encouragement like, "Oh, I'm sorry to hear that. I hope you find something soon." You probably wouldn't say, "I'm not surprised, loser. You have no business thinking anyone would want to hire someone like you."

Strangely, however, we often talk to ourselves in an abusive, overly critical manner. You might decide that failure is evidence that you're incompetent and incapable and there's no use trying again. Or even if you do try again, you might convince yourself that you're not going to succeed and consequently, you might not put in as much effort as you could.

Harsh self-criticism won't make you perform better. But self-compassion might. Self-compassion can also help you feel better.

The easiest way to practice self-compassion is simply to ask yourself, "What would I say to a friend right now?" Then give yourself those same kind words (even if you've already said some not-so-compassionate things to yourself).

WHAT YOU MIGHT SAY TO YOURSELF	WHAT YOU WOULD SAY TO A FRIEND
You're going to mess up.	Just do your best.
You shouldn't have bothered trying.	You can try again.
You embarrassed yourself.	People respect you for trying.
You're a loser for failing.	You're brave for trying.

What are some examples of harsh things you say to yourself, and how you could respond to those thoughts with kinder things you'd say to a friend? Fill in the table below.

EXAMPLES OF HARSH THINGS YOU SAY TO YOURSELF	WHAT YOU SAY TO A FRIEND

Normalize Failure

I once worked with a woman who said one of the best things her parents ever did for her was talk about failure in a positive way when she was growing up. Every Friday night, her father would ask everyone what they failed at over the course of the week. Rather than encourage them to brag about their successes, he asked each kid to share something they dared to try and failed at.

She said those weekly conversations made it OK to say she failed. If she said she failed to get the part in the play, her father would give her a big high-five for being brave enough to try out. If she said she failed a test, her father would ask her how she could try to do better next time. There was never a lecture or shaming. Instead, everyone was encouraged to do their own problem-solving for how they were going to learn from their failure.

She said, "We grew up thinking failure was proof we were doing hard things. We didn't see it as a bad thing."

Wouldn't it be great if we could all have the reassurance that failure is evidence we're brave? Well, you can begin to normalize failure in your own life by talking about your failures to other people. Start sentences with, "I fail at stuff all the time," and listen for what happens next. Those around you might feel more comfortable.

Keep in mind, you don't need to talk about huge failures. You might have plenty of small failures you can talk about too.

How can you start talking more about your failures?

_____

_____

_____

_____

_____

Who are some people you could share your failures with?

_____

_____

_____

_____

_____

_____

How can you start showing people you are proud of them for trying, not disappointed in them for failing?

_____

_____

_____

_____

_____

This Week's Homework

Think about how many times you failed this week. There may be small failures, like failing to complete a task on time. But perhaps there were some bigger failures too, like having a book proposal rejected. Remind yourself that those failures are proof that you're putting yourself out there and trying. If you haven't failed at all, it could be a sign you're not pushing yourself hard enough.

Create Your Plan to Stop Giving Up After Your First Failure

What are things you can do to stop giving up after your first failure?

☐ Identify why I want to give up and determine if quitting actually is the healthiest thing to do

☐ Study famous failures for inspiration

☐ Remind myself of my favorite personal comeback story

☐ Normalize failure

☐ Talk to myself the same way I'd talk to a friend

☐ Remind myself I can handle the uncomfortable feelings that accompany failure

☐ Try again even though it feels scary

☐ _____

Identify one small step you can take to avoid giving up after your first failure. You might need to increase your courage or push yourself to keep going even though your brain tries to convince you that you shouldn't try again. Here are some examples of small steps you might take to stop giving up after your first failure:

➤ I will talk about my failures with my friends so I don't feel ashamed when I fail or get rejected.

➤ When I fail to reach my weekly goal, I'll sit down to develop a plan I can use to try and do better next week.

➤ When I try to convince myself I shouldn't try again, I'll remember my favorite comeback story so I can build the courage to take another chance.

➤ I will reach out to ten prospective clients each week, knowing that most of them will decline. But I will keep going even if they don't respond to my invitation.

➤ I will write down my failures on a white board throughout the year. I will read those things to remind me how brave I was to put myself out there.

What's one step you can take to move forward after you fail?

_____

_____

_____

_____

_____

_____

What will you notice about yourself when you stop giving up after your first failure?

_____

_____

_____

_____

_____

_____

How will your life be different?

_____

_____

_____

_____

_____

_____

When I **STOPPED** fearing alone time . . .

I sat with all the parts of me that needed to heal. I accepted the broken parts of myself as being a source of strength as opposed to weakness, and I filled the cracks with unconditional love of self.

—Lance Kelly (35, Pennsylvania)

I realized I'm not such bad company.

—Justin R. (31, Arizona)

I stopped waiting for other people to do things with me. I learned to explore alone and I don't have to worry about whether someone else is having fun.

—Maria A. (27, Florida)

Don't
Fear
Alone
Time

THE PANDEMIC FORCED many people to spend more time alone. And while some people may have learned to grow more comfortable being by themselves, others may dislike it more than ever after being isolated from other people for such a long time.

The fear of alone time certainly predates COVID, though. Many people have struggled with this one for a long time.

Technology has created this strange sense of false connection. You might find yourself turning to social media to relieve loneliness. But over the long-term, all those online conversations might actually cause a greater sense of loneliness. That cycle often causes people to fear alone time more than ever because they equate being alone with feeling lonely. Thanks to our electronics, you never really have to be alone with your thoughts anymore. It's easy to fill every waking second with video clips, news articles, and images from social media. So while learning to be alone with your thoughts can be challenging in today's world, it's well worth the effort.

How Do You Fear Alone Time?

Learning to become more comfortable with the dialogue in your mind is really important. But if you're not there yet, don't worry. We're going to cover some strategies that can help you learn to grow more comfortable being by yourself—and we'll do it one step at a time. Before we dive into talking more about the fear of being alone and the exercises that can help, let's examine how this one plays out in your life. Take a look at the following statements and place a checkmark next to the ones that ring true to you.

☐ I avoid being alone with my thoughts at all costs.

☐ I keep background noise on when I am alone to distract me from my thoughts.

☐ When I'm physically alone, I spend most of my time on my social media.

☐ I avoid doing things or going places by myself.

☐ I spend time with people I don't enjoy because it's better than being alone.

☐ Even if there was an event I really wanted to go to, I wouldn't go unless someone else goes with me.

☐ I would rather be with people who don't treat me well or whose company I don't enjoy rather than be alone.

☐ I dislike going to sleep because it's the first time all day that I am in silence.

What's an example of a time when it felt scary to be alone?

_____

_____

_____

_____

_____

What type of thoughts did you have?

_____

_____

_____

_____

_____

How did your thoughts and feelings affect your behavior?

_____

_____

_____

_____

_____

Being Alone vs. Being Lonely

When I talk about alone time, a lot of people will tell me that they love being alone. But when I ask them what they do when they're by themselves, they'll tell me they watch TV or listen to podcasts. So while they might be physically alone, they aren't alone with their thoughts. There's a difference.

When I talk about alone time, I'm referring to the idea that you can be in a quiet place without the distractions of social media or without a TV blaring in the background. It might involve going for a walk without headphones on or it may be about meditating for a few minutes. There are lots of ways to be alone with your thoughts.

That doesn't mean that you have to be lonely, however. When you learn to become more comfortable in your own skin, you can feel better about being by yourself. You can also learn to trust that you can be good company to yourself.

Of course, being around people isn't necessarily the cure for loneliness. You can feel lonely in a crowded room or while at a family gathering. Truly connecting with people is what prevents loneliness. And to connect with people, you need to be vulnerable with them which can be hard to do.

We're social creatures. We definitely need to spend time around other humans for optimal well-being. But at the same time, it's important to strike a balance that allows us to form meaningful connections with others while also being comfortable with some solitude.

In the past, what are some ways in which you have managed feelings of loneliness? What's been helpful and what hasn't?

_____

_____

_____

_____

_____

Why Do You Fear Alone Time?

There are many possible reasons why you might find alone time scary. Understanding those reasons can help you develop a plan to get more comfortable with alone time. Take a few minutes to consider some of the reasons why you might avoid spending time by yourself. Check off all the items that sound familiar and if you think of anything that wasn't on the list, fill in the blank.

☐ I equate being alone with being lonely.

☐ I am uncomfortable with the thoughts that run through my head.

☐ I feel bad when I'm alone.

☐ My brain goes into overdrive when there's silence.

☐ I assume doing things alone won't be much fun.

☐ I've never really spent time alone with my thoughts.

☐ Daydreaming or just thinking seems like a waste of time.

☐ I'm afraid I'll look like a loser if I do things by myself.

☐ I feel anxious whenever I'm alone.

☐ _____

Lilly's Story

Whenever Lilly's boyfriend announced he had plans on the weekend that didn't involve her, she felt physically ill. She imagined herself sitting around feeling lonely and being bored when he wasn't home.

To prevent that from happening, she usually called her parents to announce that she'd be coming to their house for dinner or that she'd be spending the day with them. Her parents welcomed her with open arms anytime she wanted to visit.

When her parents went away on vacation for a few weeks and her boyfriend was going to be out of town, she experienced sheer panic. And that's what motivated her to start therapy.

She said, "It's not that I'm scared for my physical safety. It's that I'm terrified to be left alone with the thoughts inside my own head. That's not OK."

Her inner monologue was really harsh. She constantly thought she wasn't good enough, she called herself names, and she convinced herself that she couldn't handle any challenges that she might face.

It was no wonder she didn't want to be alone. She was verbally abusive toward herself. When I asked her if she would want to spend time with someone else who spoke to her the way she spoke to herself, she said she wouldn't. It was clear that our first challenge was to help her talk to herself with kindness. Once she learned how to talk to herself the same way she'd talk to a friend, she started to feel better.

She also needed confidence that she could handle feeling uncomfortable. She learned to recognize if her feelings were a friend or an enemy—an exercise you'll discover shortly. If she felt anxious, lonely, or sad while she was by herself, that was OK. She could tolerate those feelings.

We started small, though. She began spending a few minutes alone with her thoughts every day. Sometimes she simply journaled for ten minutes. At other times she just rode in the car in silence—without a podcast or music.

Over time, she challenged herself to try new things alone—like eating at a restaurant or exploring a park. Doing fun things by herself helped her see that being alone could be OK too. These regular dates with herself helped her see that alone time could actually be quite fun.

By the end of our time together, Lilly reported a new sense of inner peace. She was kinder to herself, which made being alone with her inner dialogue a lot more pleasant.

Mental Strength Exercises

Learning how to be by yourself is a skill. And fortunately, there are exercises that can help you build the mental strength you need to tolerate the uncomfortable feelings that can arise when you're alone as well as exercises that will make being alone feel more comfortable. Here are some of my favorite exercises that can help you stop fearing alone time.

Ask Yourself If Your Feelings Are a Friend or an Enemy

If you aren't used to spending time alone, there's a good chance you'll feel uncomfortable. But just because you feel uncomfortable doesn't mean you shouldn't stick with it.

Sometimes it's helpful to endure an uncomfortable emotion. But not always. That's why it's important to ask whether your emotions are a friend or an enemy.

An emotion isn't either good or bad. Yet most people think excitement is a positive emotion while anger is a negative emotion. But any emotion has the power to be positive or negative. While it may not seem like there's anything positive about an uncomfortable emotion like dread, any emotion can be an opportunity to learn something about yourself.

Excitement can be your friend when you are planning a vacation and looking forward to all the fun things you are going to do.

But it might be an enemy when you get so excited about a get-rich-quick opportunity that you overlook the risks you face.

Anger might be your friend when it helps you stand up to a social injustice. It might be an enemy when it causes you to say something mean to a loved one.

Here's an example of times when certain emotions may be a friend to someone and when they may be an enemy.

	FRIEND	ENEMY
Anger	It helped me tell my boss that we were treated unfairly.	It caused me to say something rude to the project manager and I got reprimanded.
Anxiety	It warned me when the relationship I was in was unhealthy.	It talked me out of going away for the weekend with friends because I was worried something bad would happen.
Fear	It kept me from experimenting with drugs.	It prevented me from ever trying to write a book.
Sadness	It helped me honor the loss of my grandmother.	It convinced me to stay home by myself too much.
Excitement	It made holidays more fun.	I had trouble being productive at work the whole week before vacation.

Think of times in your life when a specific emotion was a friend and when it was an enemy.

	FRIEND	ENEMY
Anger		
Anxiety		
Fear		
Sadness		
Excitement		

Now think about what emotions often get stirred up when you are alone with your thoughts. What are some of those feelings?

_____

_____

_____

_____

_____

What can you learn from those feelings? Are they a friend or an enemy in those moments?

_____

_____

_____

_____

_____

If they're a friend, embrace those feelings.

If they're an enemy, develop a plan for how to manage those emotions. Your emotions might be a sign that you need to create some changes in your life. For example, if you constantly worry about work when you are alone with your thoughts, your anxiety might be telling you something—like you could benefit from developing better boundaries with your boss, or you're a perfectionist.

What can you learn from the emotions you experience when you are alone?

_____

_____

_____

_____

_____

Are there any changes you might want to make in your life?

_____

_____

_____

_____

_____

Zoom Out

It's easy to get so zoomed in to what you have to do next that you lose sight of the big picture in your life. You might worry a lot about what you're going to wear to work that day or how you're going to get everything on your to-do list done.

Those little concerns stack up over the course of your day and take a lot of your time and mental energy. That might leave time and energy left over to think about the big picture in life.

Are you living according to your values? Do you have any goals you want to work on? Do you have any changes you want to make?

It's important to spend more time planning your life than you spend planning what you're going to do on Friday night or what you're going to wear to a wedding.

Alone time is a prime opportunity to zoom out and think about the big picture of life.

My grandmother once told me she wanted to make sure no one ever put "She meant well . . ." on her headstone. Instead, she wanted to *do well*. And she certainly did. Keeping that in mind drove her to do great things. Even into her eighties, she was knitting prayer shawls for "elderly" shut-ins.

Developing a slogan that you wouldn't want to go on your headstone might push you to keep the big picture in mind. For example, no one wants their headstone to read things like "She sure cleaned her house a lot," or "He worked so much his family never saw him."

What's something you would never want to be on your future headstone?

_____

_____

_____

_____

Now let's think about what you do want to be known for. Imagine a loved one is describing you to someone who has never met you. What would you want them to say about you?

_____

_____

_____

_____

Investing in more time alone, whether you're journaling, establishing goals for yourself, or just thinking about changes you want to make in your life, can help ensure you're doing those things you want to be known for.

What can you do during your alone time to help you meet those goals? It might involve planning, scheduling, writing in a journal, or just reflecting.

_____

_____

_____

_____

_____

> *I realized that being alone with my thoughts was like facing any other fear. I had to practice doing it. The more I practiced it, the less scary it felt.*
>
> —Emily (43, Arkansas)

Practice Small

If you don't usually spend much time alone, don't start by trying to spend three weeks in a state of solitude. Instead, start small.

- Spend two minutes sitting in silence by yourself.
- Practice mindfulness for five minutes per day.
- Write in a journal for ten minutes.
- Turn off the music in the car whenever you are at a stoplight.
- Go for a fifteen-minute walk in nature.

What are some things you can do this week to start practicing being alone with your thoughts?

_____

_____

_____

_____

_____

Schedule a Date With Yourself

You don't have to just sit at home and stare at the walls during your alone time. Instead, you can go do fun things by yourself. In fact, it's important to ensure your alone time is fun sometimes. That way, you won't reserve time alone only for those serious talks with yourself. Instead, you can have fun with yourself too.

Here are some things you could do on your own:

- Go out to dinner
- Go to the movies
- Go to a community event
- Go hiking
- Visit a museum

What is an activity you have never tried doing by yourself that you could try alone?

_____

_____

_____

_____

_____

This Week's Homework

Set aside a few minutes each day to sit in silence and see what happens. Notice any uncomfortable feelings that crop up—loneliness, anxiety, guilt, boredom, or anything else. Practice tolerating those feelings. Learning more about your feelings is a great way to get to know yourself better.

Create Your Plan to Stop Fearing Alone Time

What are some things you can do to get more comfortable with being alone?

☐ Set aside time to sit in silence every day

☐ Pay more attention to the feelings that come up when you are alone and determine if they are a friend or an enemy

☐ Schedule dates with yourself

☐ Pay attention to the thoughts that run through your head when you're alone and allow them to happen

☐ Identify what gets in the way of spending time alone

☐ Start acknowledging the benefits of alone time so you don't listen when your brain tries to convince you it's a waste of time

Identify a small step you can take to get more comfortable sitting in silence by yourself. Some examples of small steps could include:

➤ I will set aside ten minutes every evening to just sit and think.

➤ I will start writing in a journal every morning for fifteen minutes at a time so I can be alone with my thoughts.

➤ If someone declines to go to the movies with me, I'll just go by myself rather than wait until someone else wants to go.

➤ I will schedule a weekly date with myself where I will explore a new place or test out a new restaurant.

➤ I'm going to plan a weekend getaway all by myself this year.

What's one small step you could do to get more comfortable being alone?

_____

_____

_____

_____

_____

_____

What will you notice about yourself once you start spending some time alone?

_____

_____

_____

_____

_____

_____

How will your life be different?

_____

_____

_____

_____

_____

When I **STOPPED** feeling like the world owed me something . . .

I feel that I gained contentment and gratitude for what I have. I feel that you work harder and enjoy the process for things that you decide you want.

—Soheila Assar (43, California)

I knew I owed it to myself to do my best even though there were no guarantees.

—Tyson S. (36, Colorado)

I stopped trying to convince people how hard my life was. I realized that no matter how hard things had been, the world didn't need to make up for it now.

—Carly Garrison (26, Iowa)

Don't Feel the World Owes You Anything

DURING MY FIRST semester teaching college psychology classes, an angry student approached me about her grade. She had failed an assignment and she said, "I can't believe you gave me an F! I worked really hard on this." I didn't doubt that she had worked hard—but she had done the assignment completely wrong. She hadn't listened to the instructions—or read them well enough but she demanded I give her a higher score

I acknowledged her hard work and validated her frustration. I also let her know that the failed grade wasn't going to change. I graded students on their ability to show me what they were learning, not how many hours they were putting in. Later that evening, I received an email from the student's mom, insisting I change the grade. I didn't do it, of course. Hard work doesn't guarantee success.

But sometimes we think we deserve things just because we work hard. But putting in a lot of effort doesn't mean we'll get rewarded. Whenever I find myself thinking that I somehow deserve success, I am reminded that there are mothers in developing countries who spend hours every day carrying water back from the watering hole just to have enough water for her family to survive the day. There are plenty of people out there who work way harder than I do. Fortunately, when we find ourselves feeling a little entitled, there are plenty of mental strength exercises that can help.

How Do You Feel Like the World Owes You Something?

All of us likely have times when we think we are owed more than we're getting. That's not to say you shouldn't push for better treatment or work to make things better—you should. I'll explain more later in the chapter. And we'll also get into the exercises that can help you give up a sense of entitlement (even when it's a bit subtle). Before we dive into those strategies, though, let's examine how you might feel like the world owes you something sometimes. Take a look at the following statements and place a checkmark next to any that sound like you.

- ☐ I do favors for others expecting them to do the same for me.

- ☐ I believe I should receive back the same amount of kindness as I put out into the world.

- ☐ I spend a lot of time thinking about fairness.

- ☐ I get angry with people who don't seem as generous to me as I am to them.

- ☐ I act like general rules and laws don't apply to me.

- ☐ I get upset when I don't get rewarded for something I did.

- ☐ When people treat me poorly, I beg them to treat me better (rather than set boundaries with them).

What's an example of a time when you felt like the world owed you something?

_____

_____

_____

_____

_____

What were you thinking?

_____

_____

_____

_____

_____

How did your thoughts and feelings influence your behavior?

_____

_____

_____

_____

_____

Wanting a Better Life vs. a Sense of Entitlement

The idea that you shouldn't feel entitled gets a little misconstrued sometimes. I hear people say things like, "No, I *do* deserve better!"

> We all go through spells of "I don't deserve this. I deserve more" or "I should have been born rich." However, when one looks around and actually visualizes what they do have (and that is not material things) one realizes the blessings that have been bestowed upon them. There are so many others in this world that need more than what most of us do have.
>
> —Rolando Villarreal (64, Mexico)

Of course, if you are being mistreated, you deserve better. There are plenty of kind people in the world who will treat you well and you deserve to be around those people, not someone who abuses you.

Wanting a better life for yourself is a good thing. If you grew up in poverty, your goal might be to give your kids a better childhood. Or if you aren't happy with your current career, it's healthy to make a change.

Thinking the world owes you something is different. It's about believing that good things should come your way simply because you're a great person or because you've survived tough times.

People often say things to me like, "It's great you got to write a book. After losing your mother and your husband, you deserve to have good things happen to you."

Nope. Going through hardship didn't make me more deserving than anyone else. And trust me, the good things that have happened in my life didn't erase the bad. That's just life. One person isn't more deserving than others.

Of course, it's normal to cheer a little harder when we see someone overcome tough obstacles. It's great to hear a story of a homeless person who becomes a successful entrepreneur. But just because someone was homeless at one point in their lives doesn't mean they are more deserving of success down the road.

What's an example of a time in your life when you've wanted things to get better without feeling a sense of entitlement?

_____

_____

_____

_____

_____

Why Do You Feel Like the World Owes You Something?

You may have been told that good things happen to good people. Or that hard work always leads to success. Those beliefs can sometimes lead to an attitude of entitlement.

Of course, putting out good vibes into the world can lead to positive returns. If you go about your day with a smile on your face, other people are more likely to be friendly and treat you with kindness. But the positive returns you receive from being a positive person are a byproduct of your behavior. If you only put out good vibes with the sole intention of reaping a reward, you will likely be disappointed every time you don't get the return on your investment you think you deserve.

Think of how many of these statements might drive you to feel a sense of entitlement sometimes:

- [ ] I want life to be fair.
- [ ] I want control over what happens to me.
- [ ] I believe I should be compensated for being a good person.
- [ ] I think I was born to be successful.
- [ ] I believe I am special.
- [ ] I think the positive vibes I put out into the world should come back to me.
- [ ] _____.

> *I used to think things like, "Don't I just deserve to have something good happen to me today for once?" as if the bad things that happened to me the previous days made me more deserving of a positive outcome. When I quit doing that, I started taking responsibility for making it a good day, rather than waiting for someone to give me happiness.*
>
> —Craig Dennison (42, Ohio)

Lynn's Story

Lynn began therapy with me because she was feeling depressed. She had seen several therapists over the course of her life to deal with earlier trauma. She thought treatment had been helpful in the past, so she was hopeful it could help with her depression too.

Lynn was really big into what she called "the Law of Attraction." But her interpretation of the Law of Attraction was that as long as she thought about good things happening to her, the world would respond accordingly.

She had a vision board filled with images of exotic places she wanted to visit, a red sports car she wanted to own, and a beautiful home she wanted to buy. She spent a lot of time imagining herself enjoying all of those wonderful things and fully expecting all that good fortune to come her way somehow.

She wasn't taking any action to make those things happen, however. Instead, she worked a job that paid her basic living expenses. Her car had recently broken down and she didn't have enough money for repairs. So purchasing that red sports car was a far-fetched idea. But she remained convinced that she could "manifest" amazing greatness to come her way with the power of her thoughts.

Her treatment focused on helping her see that while thinking about positive things in her life wasn't bad, her thoughts didn't possess any magic. She wasn't entitled to material wealth because it was on her vision board. She had to take steps to make it happen.

One of the things we did was take a look at what she had to give the world (an exercise we'll cover later in this chapter). She created a new vision board. Instead of filling it with things she was hoping the universe would give her, she created a board that showed which gifts she could contribute to society.

She was kind, smart, and compassionate. She had a heart to help people in need, especially kids who had been through traumatic experiences. She began knitting winter hats and mittens for kids who were in foster care. She put that on her vision board because she knew she could make a difference in a child's life.

She also began visualizing herself working hard to increase her chances of success—rather than simply visualizing the universe gifting her with things.

As soon as she made that shift, she empowered herself. She began believing that she had the power to change her world and she didn't need to passively wait for the world to give her what she wanted.

By the end of her treatment, Lynn bought herself a car. It wasn't the sports car she had put on the vision board, but it was a dependable car that helped her get to work consistently. During her last session, she said, "I used to believe that the universe would gift me things. Now I believe in my ability to work hard, solve problems, and deal with disappointment."

Mental Strength Exercises

It can be tough to manage all those feelings that arise when you feel as though you aren't getting your fair share. Fortunately, there are several exercises that can help you build the mental strength you need to stop feeling like the world owes you something. Here are my favorite strategies.

Smell the Pizza

There are times when you aren't going to be treated the way you want, but that doesn't necessarily mean you are going to set a boundary. Maybe you waited on hold for a long time only to discover the person who eventually answers your call isn't able to help. Telling them you aren't going to call back again isn't going to change anything.

In those situations, you might be quick to find yourself thinking, "I deserve better than this!"

Thoughts about how you deserve better will send a flood of stress hormones into your body and fuel your belief that the world is out to get you.

A quick way to calm yourself is to "smell the pizza." Here's how it works:

1. Breathe in slowly through your nose like you're smelling a delicious piece of pizza.

2. Now breathe out slowly through pursed lips like you're cooling the pizza down.

3. Do this three times to help calm your brain and your body.

When you feel calmer, you can think more clearly. And you might be less likely to take your frustration out on those around you—even when things aren't fair.

Of course, putting out good vibes into the world can lead to positive returns. If you go about your day with a smile on your face, other people are more likely to be friendly and treat you with kindness. But the positive returns you receive from being a positive person are a byproduct of your behavior. If you only put out good vibes with the sole intention of reaping a reward, you will likely be disappointed every time you don't get the return on your investment you think you deserve.

> If someone is mistreating you, you don't deserve to be treated poorly. Whether you have an abusive boss or a mean friend, in these circumstances, the goal shouldn't be to build more mental strength so you can withstand further mistreatment. The goal should be to set boundaries and change your environment so you can become the strongest and best version of yourself. You might smell the pizza as a way to help you build the strength you need to take action.

What are some times in life when it will be helpful to stop and smell the pizza?

_____

_____

_____

_____

_____

Write Yourself a Kind Letter

Sometimes the best words of wisdom come from yourself. But it's hard to remember those kind words when you're feeling overwhelmed, stressed-out, or angry at the world.

That's where a kind letter to yourself can come into play. When you're calm, write yourself a letter that will remind you that even though your hard work won't always be recognized or you won't always be appreciated for the good things you do, you're still a great person and you can choose to keep going.

Here's a sample letter you might write to yourself:

Dear Jill,

There are going to be plenty of times when life is going to knock you down. But you have the option to get back up each time.

There's no sense in wasting your time complaining. Instead, pick up the pieces and move forward. Don't worry about keeping score and thinking about whether you're deserving of misfortune.

You're a great person and bad things are going to happen to you sometimes. Accept it, move forward, and stay strong.

Now write yourself a letter.

_____

_____

_____

_____

_____

_____

_____

_____

_____

_____

_____

_____

You may want to rewrite the letter on a piece of paper outside this workbook. Keep that letter handy—like in your desk or saved on your phone. Then read it whenever you need a little reminder that you're OK and you can get through tough times even when life isn't kind to you.

> *I continue to give back, foster kids, work at the soup kitchen, I have a big sign in my kitchen that says, "Someone else is happy with less than what you have."*
>
> —Michelle Psyck (52, North Dakota)

What Can You Give the World?

Have you ever thought about the gifts you have to give the world? Keep in mind that a gift isn't a loan. You aren't loaning the world your talents in order to be paid back with interest.

That's not to say you shouldn't charge for your time or that you should always say yes to requests for favors.

But you have an opportunity to leave an imprint on the world somehow. Being kind to other people, teaching someone something new, and sharing your talents are just a few ways you might leave the world a little better than you found it.

What do you have to offer other people? Talents, knowledge, time?

_____

_____

_____

_____

_____

How can you stay more focused on what you can give rather than what you think you deserve to receive?

_____

_____

_____

_____

_____

Pay attention to those moments when you find yourself thinking that you deserve special treatment. Are there times when you think you're more special than everyone else? Are there moments when you think you're above the rules?

Create Your Plan to Avoid Feeling Like the World Owes You Anything

What are some things you can do to stop feeling like the world owes you anything?

- ☐ Establish boundaries so I can create a healthy life for myself
- ☐ Write myself a kind letter that I can read whenever I feel entitled
- ☐ Smell the pizza to calm my brain and my body when I'm feeling entitled
- ☐ Acknowledge what I can give to the world
- ☐ Reframe my thoughts when I insist the world owes me something
- ☐ _____

Identify some concrete action steps you can take to stop feeling like the world owes you something. Here are some examples of what those steps might look like:

➤ When I find myself thinking something is unfair, I'll remind myself that it's OK for things to be unfair.

➤ I'll catch myself when I start to insist that the rules don't apply to me. And I'll challenge myself to consider why I think the rules don't apply to me.

➤ When someone mistreats me, I will establish healthy boundaries.

➤ When I insist someone owes me something, I'll remind myself that it's my choice that I helped them or gave them something.

What's one step you can take that will help you stop feeling like the world owes you something?

_____
_____
_____
_____
_____
_____

What will you notice about yourself once you stop feeling like the world owes you something?

_____
_____
_____
_____
_____
_____

How will your life be different?

_____

_____

_____

_____

_____

_____

When I **STOPPED** expecting immediate results . . .

I realized that even though I am still not there I am going to get there!!

—Bill Bamber (79, Canada)

I found I had patience I never knew before.

—Eric H. (25, Massachusetts)

I stopped being so stressed-out about everything. I relaxed my time line and realized that when things happen at a slower pace, I have a chance to learn while I wait.

—Greg Haskell (34, Washington State)

Don't
Expect
Immediate
Results

WE LIVE IN the world where you can get an answer to almost any question within a minute and you can get items delivered to your door within hours. The more technology makes things happen fast, the less patience we have when it comes to seeing results.

But personal growth happens at a much slower pace. You won't change your habits, improve your relationships, or get better at managing your emotions in an instant. And it's not just time that's required to make lasting change—you also have to sharpen your skills with practice. Fortunately, there are some strategies that can help you persist even when you aren't seeing change overnight.

How Do You Expect Immediate Results?

Whether you want to grow mentally stronger or you want to get physically healthier, the exercises in this chapter can help you stay the course. Before we get into those exercises, let's examine the ways in which you might expect immediate results. Review the following statements and place a checkmark next to ones that sound like you.

☐ I give up if I don't get the results I want right away.

☐ I overestimate how fast I am able to accomplish something.

☐ I underestimate how difficult a task is going to be.

☐ I go to unhealthy measures to speed things up sometimes.

☐ I start out doing something in full force—but then I can't sustain that energy over the long term.

☐ I imagine how much time something is going to take and I don't bother trying.

What's an example of a time when you expected immediate results?

_____
_____
_____
_____
_____

What are some thoughts you had?

_____
_____
_____
_____
_____

How were you feeling?

_____
_____
_____
_____
_____

How did those thoughts and feelings affect your behavior?

_____
_____
_____
_____

Expecting Immediate Results vs. Making Things Happen Fast

It's OK to work hard to make things happen fast. That's different from expecting immediate results.

Let's say you want to lose a hundred pounds. Expecting to do that this month is unrealistic. You can, however, start working hard to make it happen faster—hit the gym, hire a trainer, and change your diet. It might take a year to safely shed the weight, but daily hard work might get you there.

People who expect immediate results often do two things: they start out at such a high intensity that they can't sustain it long enough to see results, or they stay so focused on how long it's going to take that they forget to look at which steps they can take right now. The desperation to see fast results can also lead people to take unhealthy shortcuts that can ultimately backfire.

What's a time when you expected immediate results and it didn't work out so well for you?

_____

_____

_____

_____

_____

What's a goal you've worked on that required persistence over the long haul?

_____

_____

_____

_____

_____

Why Do You Expect Immediate Results?

There are many possible reasons why you expect immediate results. Consider how many of these sound true and if you think of anything that didn't make the list, add it to the blank line:

- ☐ I don't want to waste my time if something isn't working.
- ☐ I lack patience.
- ☐ I lose motivation fast.
- ☐ I convince myself it's going to be too hard to stick to something for a long time.
- ☐ My attempts to change are sometimes half-hearted and when I don't see immediate results, I decide something must not be working.
- ☐ I don't know which expectations are realistic.
- ☐ I want to set the bar high.
- ☐ _____

> *The impatience and the anxiety I feel when something doesn't happen fast helps me gain more confidence in myself. I now see it's my job to handle the turmoil, not speed things up.*
>
> —Warren M. (43, Florida)

Chuck's Story

Chuck came into my therapy office saying he felt stuck. His wife was most likely experiencing depression and she didn't want to do anything about it.

He said it was tough to be married to a woman who sat on the couch all the time watching TV. For over a year, he had tried to convince her to get help and she refused. He said, "When I married her I promised to stick with her in sickness and in health. But I don't think our relationship is healthy for either of us at this point."

He recognized he had taken on the role of a parent rather than a partner.

He said, "I remind her to eat. Tell her to go to bed. Encourage her to clean up and try to convince her to go do fun things. She argues back with me like a defiant teenager."

We developed a goal (something we'll cover next) for Chuck. He wanted to start communicating with his wife differently. Instead of lecturing, he could listen. And instead of pointing out what she should be doing, he could focus on the positive and try to reinforce the steps she tried. He could also invite her to do things with him without nagging or shaming her if she chose not to.

Chuck came back in the next week and said, "That didn't work. She still won't go see a doctor."

So we talked about how long it took to get into their current pattern of communication—over a year. And then we talked about how long Chuck thought it would reasonably take for things to change. He was able to step back and acknowledge it was unreasonable to think that things would miraculously change in one week.

We also discussed his expectation that his wife was going to start seeing a doctor. He couldn't control her decisions. But he could control how he communicated with her.

Once he started focusing on improving his communication, he felt relieved. He didn't need to measure "success" by whether his wife began treatment. Instead, he could measure his own success rate by looking at how many times he chose to improve his communication with his wife over the week. And each week, there were many opportunities.

Over the course of several weeks, Chuck noticed some positive changes. They were arguing less and talking more. His wife occasionally made comments about wanting to feel better and when she did, he was able to encourage her without his previous sarcastic comments.

After a few months, he invited her to join him for a therapy session and she agreed. When she came to the appointment with him, we talked about their relationship, the improvements she'd seen in Chuck lately, and how she felt. At the end of the session, she agreed to a referral to one of my colleagues so she could talk to someone about her depression.

After a few months, Chuck felt more in control of his life and more hopeful about his marriage. He focused on improving his communication while also supporting his wife's efforts in treatment. He knew that it was going to take time to heal their relationship and for her depression to improve. But he trusted that the small steps he was taking were headed in the right direction and if he kept going, he'd eventually get to his goals.

I remind myself that my goals are more like a marathon, not a sprint. I stay focused on what I can do today while also keeping my bigger overall goal in mind. I don't expect to cross the finish line today, but I do expect to get one step closer.

—Emily (32, Kansas)

Mental Strength Exercises

Expecting immediate results can be a tough habit to break. But there are many strategies that can help you develop patience, grit, and perseverance so you can reach your goals. Here are my favorite exercises that can help you stop expecting immediate results.

Establish a Healthy Goal

It's important to start with a good goal. If you start with an impossible goal, you'll sabotage your chances of success.

I see a lot of people creating goals that are impossible to achieve. If you start with an impossible goal with unreasonable expectations, you set yourself up to fail.

A slight shift in the way you create a goal can make a huge difference in ensuring you have reasonable expectations.

For example, what does it mean when you say you want to "get healthier"? If you drink more water and eat a few more vegetables, did you meet your goal? Or what if you went for a walk three days a week? Does that mean you're healthier?

Good goals should be:

Measurable: You can't measure whether you are "healthier" but you can measure if you eat five servings of vegetables and work out for twenty minutes three days per week.

Actionable: Sometimes people say things like, "I want to feel better." But it's important to identify the steps you're going to take to feel better. You might say you're going to take thirty minutes each day to do something you enjoy. The side effect of that behavior is that you might feel better.

Doable: Create a goal that you have control over. So rather than declare that you want to get promoted, say which steps you're going to take to try and earn a promotion (go to two networking events per month, take a class, volunteer to take on one extra project per week, etc.).

UNHELPFUL GOAL	HELPFUL GOAL
I want to be happier.	I'll start scheduling three fun things to do each week.
I want to have a better social life.	I'll join two new clubs or activities this month to meet some people.
I want to get in shape.	I'll walk 5 nights a week for 30 minutes.
I want to take better care of myself.	I'll start doing one thing to take care of myself every Saturday afternoon.
I want to have more money in the bank.	I'll start saving $100 from every paycheck.

What's an example of an unreasonable goal you've set for yourself? What made that goal unreasonable? How did it impact your expectations of when you should see results?

_____

_____

_____

_____

_____

What's a goal you can set for yourself that is measurable, actionable, and doable?

_____

_____

_____

_____

Track Your Progress, Not Your Speed

When I was in the third grade, my teacher told my mom I was really fast at getting my work done. I took that as a badge of honor. And I wanted to secure my reign as the fastest work-completer in the class. Whenever we got a worksheet, I raced through it as quickly as I could so that I could proudly deliver it to the teacher first. One of my friends decided to compete with me to see who could turn in our papers faster. That meant I had to scribble my answers more quickly than ever.

While I successfully managed to hand in my paper "first" sometimes, the quality of my work suffered. And we got graded on our work, not the speed at which we turned it in.

When my grades declined, my mom had a talk with me. She explained there was no prize for getting my work done fast. Scribbling my answers and sprinting to the teacher's desk was a bad idea. I was better off taking my time and double-checking my answers so I could learn the information.

I'd like to say I have conquered this desire to get things done fast. But, I haven't! While some people struggle to get things done because they want them to be perfect, I go for quantity over quality in lots of areas of my life to this day. Take writing, for example. I can easily write a chapter of a book in a day. It's not a good chapter—but I can do it. And as soon as it's done, I want to move on to the next chapter. Researching and writing is fun to me. Editing isn't so fun because I have to go back and fix the typos in a much slower manner. So I still have to remind myself to work on tracking true progress—not the speed at which I produce work.

It sounds ridiculous now, but it's incredibly easy to lose sight of our actual goals. Sometimes we begin to pay more attention to the speed at which we're advancing rather than the actual goal itself. Learning to track your progress—and not your speed—can help.

When organizations have a huge fundraising goal, they often create one of those giant thermometer displays and color it in as they grow closer to their goal. That's wise. It breaks down what seems like an impossible task—like raising a million dollars—into smaller steps. When you see you've reached a milestone, like you've raised fifty thousand dollars, that goal of a million feels just a little more doable.

Tracking your progress toward your goals can help you see that you're making progress, even if it's slow progress. And seeing some results can help you stay on track.

Keep in mind that what you need to track might not necessarily be the results. Instead, you might choose to track your behavior. For example, you might decide that you're going to track how often you exercise (as opposed to your weight). You can control the frequency in which you choose to work out.

You could mark an X on the calendar each day you squeeze in twenty minutes of cardio. Just looking at the calendar and how many days you are working out can help you stay on track.

A helpful strategy can involve looking at a goal for the next thirty days. You can accomplish a lot in those thirty days if you make something a top priority.

A couple of years ago I set out to try and get six-pack abs in twenty-eight days. I hired a trainer, changed my diet, and got to work lifting weights. I worked really hard even though I wasn't convinced I was going to make it happen. But by the end of the month, I reached my goal. I had six-pack abs that impressed my trainer enough that he hired a photographer to take the "after" photos that he could show to the world.

In hindsight, "getting six-pack abs" probably wasn't the best goal. There were some serious variables I couldn't control (apparently, genetics play a big role in whether your ab muscles actually show). A better goal would have been something like, "I'm going to work out with a trainer six days a week and follow the recommended diet plan."

I learned that you can get some amazing results when you make something a top priority. But most of the time in life, the things we want to accomplish aren't necessarily worthy of becoming our top priority. Your relationships, your mental health, your social life, and your finances may need to take precedence. If something lands on your priority list somewhere around number five, know that it's going to take some time to see results.

So if your overall goal is to pay off twenty thousand dollars in debt, think about what you can realistically pay down in the next month. You might decide to set a goal to pay off two thousand dollars to start and begin developing a strategy to help you with that.

What's a goal you can work on in the next thirty days?

_____

_____

_____

_____

_____

How can you track your progress?

_____

_____

_____

_____

_____

Prove Your Brain Wrong

As you start working on a big goal, your brain will try to convince you to quit. It will tell you that you're too tired, that your goal is too ambitious, or you can't possibly overcome whatever obstacle stands in your way.

It will also try to convince you that what you're doing isn't working. It will tell you that your efforts are being wasted and there's no use in trying.

Fortunately, your brain isn't always right. In fact, its job is to convince you to play it safe and take it easy in life. Your job is to prove your brain wrong. When it tells you that you can't do something, consider it a challenge. Then put everything you have into proving your brain wrong.

> When I think about a big goal, I get tired. But when I focus on what I can do now, I feel energized. So I try to focus more on what I can accomplish today rather than what I want to accomplish in one year.
>
> —Alyson (27, Wisconsin)

Almost every day, I run a mile as fast as I can. Even though I've been doing this for years, my brain still tries to convince me to slow down on every single run. When I get to about three quarters of a mile in, my brain tells me I can't possibly keep up my speed until the finish line. It tries to convince me that I need to stop and catch my breath.

Fortunately, I know my brain underestimates me. When I start thinking those thoughts, I do my best to run even faster (but that doesn't always happen). My goal is to show my brain that I can run faster even though I'm tired and I can tolerate how uncomfortable it feels when I'm gasping for air and my legs feel like they're on fire.

Of course, there are times when you need to listen to your brain. If I injure myself, I will stop running. But when I know my brain is just trying to keep me comfortable and it's healthy to keep going, I push myself.

Proving your brain wrong can help you persist for the long haul. It can help you keep going even when you don't feel like it. By now, I realize that just because my brain tells me to quit, it doesn't mean I need to. I don't have to believe those thoughts. Instead, I can remind myself that my brain underestimates me.

Physical activities are one of the best ways to prove your brain wrong. Your brain will try to convince you that you can't go on long before you actually need to quit. So while running a timed mile every day is one way you can do this, there are definitely other things you can try. Here are some examples:

Do push-ups or chin-ups. Notice the point at which your brain tells you that you can't do any more and try to do at least one more.

Go for a distance walk or jog. Pay attention to those times when your brain tells you that you're too tired to keep walking. Keep going a little farther.

Run as fast as you can. You can time yourself for a mile run like I do or you might time yourself for one lap around the track—and then try to run another lap even faster.

If you can't do a physical challenge, there are lots of other ways to prove your brain wrong. Challenge yourself to keep doing something longer than your brain says you can, like reading a book, writing in your journal, or doing breathing exercises.

What is an activity you can do to test all the ways in which your brain will tell you to quit long before you need to?

_____

_____

_____

_____

_____

What can you say to your brain when it tries to talk you out of persisting? Which steps can you take to keep going?

_____

_____

_____

_____

_____

Pay attention to all the ways you expect immediate results this week. It might be small things—like expecting an immediate response to an email. Or it might be big things, like expecting a prescription to immediately lower your cholesterol. Notice how you respond when those things don't happen as fast as you like. Are you tempted to quit? Do you get upset? Or are you able to shift your expectations in a healthy way?

Create Your Plan to Stop Expecting Immediate Results

What are some things you can do to stop expecting immediate results?

☐ Adjust my expectations

☐ Establish realistic goals

☐ Find ways to track my progress

☐ Practice proving my brain wrong

☐ Focus on patience, rather than immediate results

☐ _____

Now identify a few small steps you can take to stop expecting immediate results. These strategies might involve shifting your mindset as well as changing your behavior so you can keep working toward your goals even when things aren't happening as fast as you like. Here are a few examples of small steps you might take to stop expecting immediate results:

➤ I will establish a monthly financial goal and a small objective I can work on meeting every day.

➤ I will track my fitness goals based on how many days I work out so I don't worry about the exact weight loss I experience.

➤ I will talk to my doctor about what I can realistically expect to see for results with my medication and I will chart my progress once per week.

➤ I will spend thirty minutes every day listening to a financial podcast so I can learn more about money over the course of three months.

➤ When I am tempted to quit learning how to speak another language, I'll remind myself of how much I have learned already instead of focusing on how much more I have to learn.

What's one step you can take that will help you stop expecting immediate results?

_____

_____

_____

_____

_____

_____

What will you notice about yourself once you stop expecting immediate results?

_____

_____

_____

_____

_____

_____

How will your life be different?

_____

_____

_____

_____

_____

_____

Conclusion

READING A BOOK about physical strength exercises won't give you big muscles. Similarly, completing a workbook about mental strength won't make you mentally strong. But practicing the mental strength exercises on a regular basis will help you grow stronger.

Keep in mind that developing mental muscles is an ongoing process. Take a break for a while, and your muscles will atrophy.

Sometimes I hear people say things like, "I don't need to build mental strength. I'm strong already." But just like your physical muscles need ongoing exercise, so do your mental muscles.

You'll likely find some exercises become your go-to strategies. You can mix and match exercises from the chapters to tackle various issues. Writing yourself a kind letter or smelling the pizza, for example, might help you stop feeling sorry for yourself as well as help you avoid giving up after your first failure. Someone else might find that calling themselves by name and talking to themselves like a good friend works best in those situations.

It's up to you to decide which exercises help you grow into the strongest and best version of yourself.

And, of course, the exercises will only work if you're taking care of yourself and creating the healthiest environment possible so you can thrive.

Recall Tough Times You've Been Through Before

No matter what kind of challenge you face, an exercise that can always help is to recall the inner strength that has helped you get through tough times in the past. Recalling how you got through other hard times will remind you how much inner strength you have already.

Whenever I find myself filled with self-doubt or questioning whether I can accomplish something, I remember what I've survived in the past.

I used to be terrified of public speaking. The thought of speaking in front of a roomful of people seemed unthinkable. But I gave the eulogy at Lincoln's funeral. In that moment, I didn't care if my voice shook or I said something wrong. Instead, my goal was to tell Lincoln's story, and I wanted everyone in the room to hear it. There were many things that helped me get through it, such as my faith, my friends, my family, and the conversations I had with myself about working through my grief.

Now, whenever I'm scared to do something or I'm doubting my ability to handle hardship, I remind myself that if I survived the loss of my husband—and I found the courage to speak at his funeral—I can get through whatever challenge is in front of me right now.

While I don't know your story, I'm sure you've survived something tough in your life, too. You've probably gotten through hard things that you wouldn't have thought possible.

I want you to pick one. Pick the hardest thing you ever went through and think about how you managed to get through it. Write your story now and remember it whenever you're struggling with something. Include details about how you got through that tough time. That story will remind you that you have inner strength that at the time you didn't even know you had. And if you can get through that, you can get through whatever you're going through now—or whatever challenge you face down the road.

My Inner-Strength Story

Develop Your Plan

Think about which steps you're going to take to keep building mental strength in your life.

But before you do, think about which counterproductive bad habits you're going to focus on giving up. You don't have to work on all 13 things at once. Instead, pick one bad habit you want to tackle first. It might be the one that you do the most often or the one you're struggling with the most right now.

Which of the 13 things are you going to work on first? What made you pick that thing to tackle first?

_____

_____

_____

_____

_____

_____

_____

_____

Which exercises are you going to use to address it?

_____

_____

_____

_____

_____

_____

_____

_____

_____

How will you know when you're growing mentally stronger? What changes will you see?

_____

_____

_____

_____

_____

_____

_____

_____

Which warning signs will indicate to you that you need to work harder on building mental strength?

_____

_____

_____

_____

_____

_____

_____

_____

_____

If you're struggling to build mental strength on your own, what steps can you take?

_____

_____

_____

_____

_____

_____

_____

Become Your Own Mental Strength Coach

My personal journey has taught me that I'm stronger than I thought. And even though pushing myself to do hard things is uncomfortable, it's also the key to living my best life.

Of course, I'm still a work in progress. There are plenty of days when I give in to temptations or when I believe my unhelpful thoughts. But now I have the skills to learn from my mistakes and the courage to keep moving forward.

Just like me, I'm sure there will be times when you feel strong and times when you don't. There will be seasons of your life that seem easy and seasons that feel like a constant challenge.

You might struggle with one issue at one time and a completely different issue at another. Life's inevitable ups and downs will test your strength from all directions.

Fortunately, you can become your own mental strength coach throughout it all. Check in with yourself to see how you're doing.

At the end of every day ask yourself, "What did I do today to become mentally stronger?" There are a lot of things that will happen to you each day that will be out of your control. But you can control how you respond to those things. There are many opportunities each day to give up the unhealthy habits that can hold you back and many chances to practice the exercises that will help you grow mentally stronger.

So whether you spoke up even though you felt scared or you resisted a temptation that could have derailed you from your goals, acknowledge what you did every day to build mental strength. Recognizing the steps you are taking each day to grow stronger will help you see the progress you're making over time.

There are several things you can do to make asking yourself this question a daily habit. Write in a journal, ask yourself while brushing your teeth before bed, or tell your partner over dinner each evening. Whatever you choose to do, incorporating this into your daily life can ensure that you make mental strength-building a key part of your overall plan to live your best life.

What's something you've done today to grow mentally stronger?

_____

_____

_____

_____

_____

How can you remind yourself to ask that question every day?

_____

_____

_____

_____

_____

Your struggles are a sign that certain skills may need a little sharpening. There may be times when you change course and times when you need a complete overhaul. But through it all, how you respond to whatever life throws your way is up to you.

There may be times when you decide to ask for help. An outside perspective can go a long way toward helping you feel better and grow stronger. So whether you confide in a friend, talk to your doctor, or meet with a therapist, remember that asking for help is a sign of strength, not weakness.

Keep practicing the exercises you've learned in this workbook. No matter what your goals are and no matter which challenges you face, when you let go of the things that are holding you back you can accomplish some incredible feats.

Resources

VerywellMind.com—This is the biggest mental health site in the world. I happen to be their editor in chief. Our medical review board ensures that each article is factually correct, and we offer free content that can help you learn about mental health issues and live your best life.

The Verywell Mind Podcast—I host a twice-weekly show that focuses on strategies for building mental strength. Every Monday I interview a guest who shares their tips for becoming mentally stronger. Every Friday I share a quick ten-minute episode that explains an exercise for building mental strength.

Talkspace—If you're looking for an online therapist or you want to meet with a psychiatrist who can prescribe medication, try Talkspace. I personally tested it and was impressed by the quality of treatment they offer. You can meet with a therapist via video chat or you can talk to someone via messaging throughout the week.

Headspace—Headspace is an app that teaches meditation and mindfulness strategies. In just a few minutes a day, they'll walk you through a meditation that can help you relax your brain and boost your happiness. They even have guided meditations that can help you sleep better.

Psychology Today—This site offers helpful content, including a directory of therapists. By entering your zip code, you can find local therapists who are accepting new patients. Read their bio, review their picture, and see how to schedule an appointment.

Books Written by Other Mental Health Professionals

Set Boundaries, Find Peace by Nedra Glover Tawwab

Maybe You Should Talk to Someone by Lori Gottlieb

Detox Your Thoughts by Andrea Bonior

Unwind Your Anxiety by Dr. Jud Brewer

Get Out of Your Own Way by Mark Goulston

The Body Keeps the Score by Bessel van der Kolk

How to Change by Katy Milkman

References

Chapter 1

Chorpita, Bruce F., and John R. Eeisz. *Match-ADTC: Modular Approach to Therapy for Children and Anxiety, Depression, Trauma, or Conduct Problems.* Satellite Beach, FL: PracticeWise, 2009.

Chapter 6

Maik Bieleke, Lucas Keller & Peter M. Gollwitzer (2020): If-then planning. *European Review of Social Psychology.*

Chapter 7

Wegner, D. M., Schneider, D. J., Carter, S. R., & White, T. L. (1987). Paradoxical effects of thought suppression. *Journal of Personality and Social Psychology*, 53(1), 5–13.

Chapter 10

Lin-Siegler, X., Ahn, J. N., Chen, J., Fang, F.-F. A. & Luna-Lucero, M. (2016). "Even Einstein Struggled: Effects of Learning about Great Scientists' Struggles on High School Students' Motivation to Learn Science." *Journal of Educational Psychology, 108*(3), 314–28.

Acknowledgments

IT'S BEEN A dream to revisit the original *13 Things Mentally Strong People Don't Do* and expand upon each of the things with this workbook. I'm honored that HarperCollins recognized the importance of this project.

I am grateful to Lisa Sharkey at HarperCollins, who has believed in me and my books since the beginning. She has been instrumental in turning my ideas about mental strength into books.

Many thanks to the rest of the dedicated team at HarperCollins, including Maddie Pillari and Emilia Marroquin, for their assistance.

I'm also grateful for my agent, Stacey Glick, who encouraged me to turn my article "13 Things Mentally Strong People Don't Do" into a book. And she's supported every project since that time.

Of course, my biggest thank-you goes to my readers, social media followers, and podcast listeners. Thank you for asking your questions, buying my books, and showing an ongoing interest in learning more about mental strength. You've made my journey possible. And a special thank-you to all the readers who supplied me with me quotes and tips for this workbook. I appreciate you.

About the Author

AMY MORIN is a licensed clinical social worker and psychotherapist, and the editor in chief of Verywell Mind, the biggest mental health website in the world. She's the host of *The Verywell Mind Podcast*, on which she offers weekly tips for building mental strength and interviews celebrities, experts, and authors about their strategies for being mentally strong.

With more than twenty-one million views, her TEDx talk, "The Secret of Becoming Mentally Strong," is one of the most viewed TEDx talks of all time. She's a highly sought-after keynote speaker who has delivered talks to companies and conferences around the globe. Her books have sold more than one million copies and been translated into more than forty languages. She lives on a sailboat in the Florida Keys.